G R FOR A THE C E

W O R K P L A C E

G R <small>FOR</small> A <small>THE</small> C E
W O R K P L A C E

MONDAY MORNING INCENTIVE

PAUL G. JOHNSON

EcceNova Editions
Victoria BC

For copyright licenses, please contact: Access Copyright, 1 Yonge Street, Suite 1900, Toronto ON M5E 1E5.

Library and Archives Canada Cataloguing in Publication

Johnson, Paul G. (Paul Gordon),1931-
  Grace for the workplace : monday morning incentive / Paul G. Johnson.

Includes bibliographical references and index.
ISBN 0-9735341-0-9

    1. Grace (Theology) 2. Work—Religious aspects—Christianity.
3. Management—Religious aspects—Christianity. I. Title.

BT738.5.J64 2004   261.8'5   C2004-903148-1

WHAT PEOPLE ARE SAYING ABOUT
GRACE FOR THE WORKPLACE

"Paul Johnson is blessed with a rare and robust grasp upon the good news of God's lavish and liberating grace. How well he perceives that divine wrath is not merely tempered, but absolutely trumped by the mercy of God. In his writing, truth and grace put in a timely appearance, apparent in the contrast between the strength of his ideas and the mild manner of presenting them.

What he wants to do is build a most ambitious bridge between worship life and work life. By observing how we are more likely to discuss faith at work than we are to discuss work within our faith communities, Johnson sets before us a compelling challenge to change focus.

Recently, I drove north in the long, gleaming tunnel under the city of Boston, newly created by the so-called 'big dig'. What amazed me most about this underground journey was bursting forth, finally, onto a spectacular new bridge. *Grace for the Workplace* offers a parallel experience."

William E. Braun, Pastor
St. Luke Lutheran Church, Devon, Pennsylvania

"This spiritual gem is theologically grounded and rooted in scripture. ... Pastor Johnson's thought-provoking ideas about the human propensity for law, leadership models, preaching, learning and the primacy of grace will raise the bar on what you expect from work and from the pulpit." *...Read more on pg. 118*

Keith Perleberg, Roman Catholic Priest
Diocese of Madison, Wisconsin

"[Johnson] challenges Christians in general, and clergy in particular, to rediscover the central place that a theology of grace should occupy in our faith. ... He offers some intriguing parables of workplace theology and encourages us to mature in our spiritual understanding as we consider how the love of God can operate in an increasingly secular world." ...*Read more on pg. 22*

Alfred C. Acer, Pastor, Reformation Lutheran Church, West Long Branch, New Jersey

"In forty years I have never once heard the word 'capitalism' mentioned in church. Yet, it is the air I breathe every day. The author admits that losing a sale is more a sin against stockholders than against God, but with gentle irony he adds that wherever support in the midst of failure shows up, the undeserved nature of grace has appeared. I've never read words like that. It's as if the workplace was God's habitat. An awesome idea." ...*Read more on pg. 48*

Cindy Zafft, doctoral candidate employed by the World Education Corporation

"Johnson helps active pastors and seminarians preparing for parish ministry to apply Bonhoeffer's idea that God is in the center of the weekday world. ... I wish I had read this book fifty years ago. Good thing that I am saved by grace, too." ...*Read more on pg. 68*

Gordon S. Nelson, Retired Pastor. West Barnstable, Massachusetts

"The challenge has been made and the tools provided. All that is needed is acceptance. A 'must read' for management." ...*Read more on pg. 90*

Robert Kondracki, former Principal at Southeastern Massachusetts Vocational Technical School

"Thank you for your prod to spread the good news in every part of our lives." ...*Read more on pg. 117*

Lauren J. Holm, RN, MSN Staff Specialist Massachusetts General Hospital

"Grace for the Workplace is a refreshing concept that links Sunday worship with Monday morning duties. The author is surely right in suggesting that many pew sitters have employment positions that could support and encourage the concept of grace taking hold. The book provides a helpful operational definition of grace to those of us in the corporate world.

In retrospect, I can see where grace has been at work, enabling me to be successful in empowering people. Still, change in the corporate culture is a long term process, and along the way there is much need for the forgiving nature of grace."

Rick Anderson, Plant Manager
Boeing Aircraft Corporation,
Seattle, Washington

"What a thought-provoking book. The separation of law versus grace, especially by the clergy and within the church, was a new concept to me. The examples made it very clear just how long this struggle has been going on.

I was a manager in a company driven by the laws and hierarchy of authority. Decisions were made by the CEO behind closed doors and handed down. Information was delivered to employees on a need-to-know basis.

I was also manager at one of those rare companies that attempt to bring some grace to the workplace. Yes, there were performance reviews, and raises were based upon perceived performance. But this company worked very hard, from the CEO on down, to ensure that all employees were considered equally important. Everyone was encouraged to make decisions, and speak directly to the CEO. Closed offices did not exist. People were trusted to be honest, and hard working, and to do what was right for the company. Management's challenge was to provide employees with the opportunities and environment to demonstrate their strengths. Deming's ideas were taken seriously and implemented. What I did not realize at the time was that this was a form of grace from the top management. I wish I had recognized this far sooner. As both an employee and a manager I was a recipient of this grace. I will forever appreciate having worked in this environment.

My challenge is to bring the concept of grace to my current workplace, to try to instill some of these ideas at all levels of management. I'm going to buy a few copies of this book to give to my manager friends... and maybe drop a couple off on the top management's desks!"

Dave Hempstead
Research and Development Software Manager
Andover, Massachusetts

ACKNOWLEDGMENT

I've had e-mail capability for a number of years but until recently I was not even curious how this amazing bit of technology worked. I took it for granted. I only knew it saved on postage and envelopes. Then came the editorial phase of this book, and the need for constant correspondence with my publisher in Victoria, British Columbia, Canada, over three thousand miles away from where I live. Were it not for e-mail capability, this book might not have been published. It took over a week each way to converse by snail mail, whereas pushing the "send" button immediately crossed the continent. But how?

Upon asking a computer technician, I learned that there is something called a Universal Linking System throughout the US and the world. Every computer with e-mail capability and a modem ties into this system and messages move over fiber-optic cables in the ground, or above it, to their destination. The oceans are crossed thanks to cables thirty inches in diameter that are beneath the surface of the sea.

I felt the need to express my gratitude to those nameless individuals who invented, manufactured, and continue to service this extraordinary System. It brings to mind the first words of Alexander Graham Bell when, upon inventing the telephone, he asked his accomplice, "What has God wrought?"

TABLE OF CONTENTS

A Parable : Table Talk

A CEO WALKED INTO his office for the beginning of his day only to find an envelope with his name on it laying on the desk blotter. His secretary had not put it there but he opened it anyway and found these words on a piece of paper: "Let grace enter the workplace."

He thought of several possible meanings to the word grace—a woman's name, grace notes in music, and gracefulness in sports, to name a few. However, he thought, there must be more to it. "What I need is input from others."

At noon, the CEO went to lunch in the cafeteria and deliberately chose a table where all the chairs, except one, were occupied. "May I sit here?" he asked, and with a little trepidation the workers nodded and he sat down. His intention was to tell them about the note and ask them what they thought the word "grace" might mean, and so he did just that.

One worker said it could be a prayer before eating, but others discounted that since anyone could do that, privately, if so inclined. There was no law against it.

When another alluded to the possibility of a woman named Grace showing up seeking employment, he said, "Yes, that is a possibility," but he really did not think that was what the note was about.

Although it was a bit of a stretch, a third lunch-eater wondered, perhaps hopefully, if it might refer to the company being willing to loan money to employees if the thirty day grace period ran out on health care insurance premiums. Given the cost of health care, it would have been a welcome policy addition.

When another person injected the thought that perhaps the note writer wanted the company to show reruns of the TV series *Grace under Fire*, it brought a chuckle from others at the table.

As if waiting for someone else to say it, the one who had mentioned the table prayer idea said "I've heard the word 'grace' in church hymns, and it often seems associated with the notion of forgiveness," but she added, before anyone could ridicule her for mentioning it, "I don't see what that would have to do with our workplace."

This seemed to open the door to another religious possibility. "In the Bible there are references to *unconditional* grace," a young man said, "but that, too, seems less than relevant to where we work."

The CEO, sensing there might be a churchgoer at the table, asked if anyone had ever heard a sermon refer to "grace," but none of them had. He finished his lunch, thanked the group for letting him barge in, and excused himself. He had some other possible meanings to consider now but he was at a loss as to where to go with what was taking shape in his mind. What escaped him was that he let grace momentarily enter the workplace by seeking out the perceptions of his employees.

The first thing the CEO did upon returning to his office was to look up the word "grace" in a dictionary. The table talk variety showed up, but one definition that caught his eye was "the unmerited love and favor of God toward people."

EVERY DAY, FIFTY-TWO WEEKS a year, the world's workforce travels on a treadmill of demands and accountability enforced by periodic performance reviews. On Sunday, a portion of that group settles into the pews and listens to homilies that often admonish them to greater Christian responsibility. The same people, in two different worlds, are subjected to the demands of "law." Occasionally, on Sunday, there are reassuring words, but the nagging connotation to the word "preach" lingers.

Even if the unmerited grace of God is part of someone's faith, should that person be participating in the workplace, the necessity of concentrating on assigned work tasks suppresses it. The exception is when grace is built into the managerial/labor relationship (Chapters 2 and 7). Indeed, one aim of this book is to encourage such rapport by providing business managers and employees with an expanding vision of the benefits of grace in the workplace.

There are corporations where this is already functioning. Grace has slipped into some workplaces unannounced and unacknowledged, but once there, it makes itself right at home, as if it belonged there all the time, *and it does.*

VOLUMES OF EVIDENCE

One reason the demands of law echo in church is their presence in designated biblical sermon texts (called the "lectionary") taken from the four Gospels. I had a feeling this was true, but in reading the Gospel assignments for 2004, I found that the *Revised Common Lectionary* (Series C) offers twenty-one Gospel passages that contain either law or judgment, while those that point implicitly or explicitly to God's graciousness add up to five.[1] Thus, forty percent of the time the texts set us up for bad news. Sixteen Sundays the Gospel shares with us events in the life of Jesus, which tend to be biographical in tone. There are six on other teachings and four on miracles.

In churches such as Roman Catholic, Anglican, and Lutheran, ecclesiastical authority mandates the use of lectionary texts, whereas in other Protestant group, it is optional. Where prescribed it becomes a kind of "pulpit Bible," a conscience to the preacher not to be tampered with. They make other texts that contain good news from the Gospels or the Letters seem like an intrusion. Preachers need some liberation from this.

Some professional theologians are quick to disagree. They maintain the lectionary guarantees that all facets of Scripture will be covered, as if all the chapters in the Bible were created equal. Where law texts dominate grace ones, this becomes a kind of legalism imposed on the clergy. It takes the love out of law and the joy out of grace. When pastors are allowed, or encouraged, to emphasize grace, preaching takes on a more fulfilling purpose. Sharing good news is a pleasant task.

What now can be seen as reflecting this law overdose was discovered some years ago, when a research organization from Minneapolis published its findings on what people believe.[2] Respondents were asked to answer "Agree," "Disagree," or "Uncertain" to a sizable number of statements. One of them read: "The main emphasis in the Gospel is God's rules for right living." Two-thirds of the respondents said they agreed with that statement. This was significant because the respondents were all church-attending Lutherans. In Martin Luther's own front yard unearned grace was replaced by something like the Ten Commandments.

Perhaps one-third of the above associate the grace of God with Christianity, but two-thirds have internalized "Thou shalt not" as the cornerstone of faith. Law becomes the model for many church schoolteachers and for parental discipline. It transfers from generation to generation, and crosses denominational boundaries.

In July of 2004, several polls (CNN, Gallup, and USA Today) unwittingly illustrated the scope of the law orientation in organized religion when they revealed how folks who often attend church are inclined to be conservative on social issues, while those who seldom or never attend are more inclined to be open to social justice issues. Law and moralism are wedded to each other and the data suggest that moralism lurks behind the scenes in many church worship settings. African American churches are the exception.

Corroborating evidence comes from a different source, that of a bishop in Sweden who wrote a book about one parish and its trail of five pastors. They all had access to a lectionary and we can assume they tuned into it early, in preparation for the following Sunday's homily. The title of the book, written by Bishop BoGiertz, captures the law issue we are lifting up. It was *The Hammer of God.*

Not surprisingly, when Swedish Lutheran clergy came to America the sound of the hammer soon could be heard in Minnesota, New York, and on the plains of Nebraska. However, when fifty of them who were retiring were asked to reflect on their pulpit years, many related how, if they were to live their lives over again, they would devote more sermon time to unmerited grace. That they did not feel they could do so during their career years shows that ecclesiastical authority weighed more heavily on the minds of conscientious clergy than the scripture emphasis on grace.

The book you have begun to read encourages a greater use of Scripture passages in preaching, and will provide a rationale for why. It will illustrate how the Bible itself places more importance on grace even though law examples are more plentiful.

A DIRECT LINE TO THE WORKPLACE

It happens every Sunday. A portion of the workplace occupies the pews in church, giving any preacher a potential contact with that realm where the majority of his/her parishioners spend most of their weekday time. Yet, when I was in an active preaching ministry, I made no mention of the workplace apart from a word about Labor Day, in September. On that Sunday, members were invited to bring some symbol of where they worked and place it on the altar. The altar area filled up fast. Others wore their symbols. Then, at an appropriate place in the service, we invoked God's blessing on daily work. After that brief allusion to the workplace, the subject never came up again that year, as I recall, even though Luther spoke of it as God's way of providing for the members of a society, and I was a Lutheran pastor.

The absence of pulpit forays into the workplace also crosses denominational lines. An organization of leading pulpiteers, known as the Academy of Preachers, features a different one each month giving a workshop on homiletics. Their 2004-5 list of topics included multi-culturalism and the city, but there was not one on the workplace, even though the pews are only a few yards from where they stand and deliver showcased homilies.

I have no interest in cranking up a greater measure of weekday responsibility. I am not exhorting anyone to see the workplace as a secular field of souls waiting to be harvested. I am interested in grace related to the workforce. By calling attention to where it is already present, the difference it can make speaks for itself. Grace has a workplace dimension as well as a personal one.

Clergy are at least aware of undeserved grace because of hours devoted to reading about grace in theological schools, taking notes on grace, perhaps writing papers on it, and encountering it in tests. The laity does none of this, and so most have no such awareness. The law-oriented workplace is their theological school.

GRACE IN THE GOSPELS

Jesus never used the word "grace." One Gospel reports that "the law came through Moses, grace and truth came through Jesus," but those were John's words, not Jesus'. The meaning of grace is *implicit* in at least three texts that appear in the lectionary: the Parables of the Prodigal Son, the Vineyard Owner, and Jesus urging Peter to forgive the same person seventy times seven (Chapters 9 and 10).

Taking a cue from Jesus, we should note here how the chapter, "The Boss and the Foreman" is a parable. The content is the atonement, the interaction between God and Jesus on the cross. When it is read in context, I think it will not seem inappropriate. Some might even see it as an antidote to the poison in the *Passion of Christ* movie.

Then, too, when some Gospel texts allude to law, they show Jesus denouncing the legalism of the Pharisees. However, whenever Gospel texts that focus on law and judgment are read, and they are always read, good news is not heard. Even in the crucifixion and resurrection grace is implicit. To be understood and appreciated, the grace dimension needs to be articulated (Chapters 6 and 10).

Announcing a reading as the "Gospel for the Day" can cause confusion when the only content is a threat or a warning. And since it is assumed that pew sitters know the difference between gospel with the small "g" (grace) and Gospel with the large "G" (the books), the confusion is perpetuated.

THE FOCUS OF PAUL

The clarity on unearned grace found in the writings of Paul is an underused resource for sermons on the subject. His words are the gospel within the Gospel, an *obbligato* to the first four New Testament books. His focus reflects his historic about-face: murdering Christians one day and being an unofficial apostle for Jesus the next. Paul was exhibit "A" that grace is trump. So weighty was the law and grace contrast in his mind, it motivated him to think through the implications of grace more than anyone else up to and beyond his time.

In Galatians 1:11-12, Paul underscores how the gospel was not something he concocted or received from the apostles. Being brought from legalistic zealotry to being a recipient of eternal pardon struck him as a divine gift. In Second Corinthians (3:7-10), he asserts how, compared to grace, law "has no splendor at all." In Ephesians (2:13-16), he observes that Christ "abolished the law with its commandments and ordinances" by replacing it with a relationship to himself. And in Romans (3:19-26), God's righteousness is not law and wrath, but forgiveness. We shall highlight the law/grace contrast whenever it is apropos.

Perplexing as it may be, the rarity of unearned grace in the lectionary is reflected in Christian history. For nearly 1,500 years Paul's theology was in eclipse; the Dark Ages were followed by centuries of clouds. It might seem that Luther's emphasis on "grace alone" would have resurrected Paul's focus, but like a lightning flash at night, grace in the Reformation illuminated the landscape but momentarily.

This is partly due to Luther's separating law and grace into two realms—law covering life here and now, and grace the hereafter (Chapter 4). Thus, in the 2003 movie *Luther*, grace was not mentioned once, though it greatly affected the reformer. However, it is also due to the German theologian, Dietrich Bonhoeffer, who, without realizing it, buried grace under the shroud of a penitential condition. His brief reference to "cheap grace" has relegated unearned favor to the ecclesiastical archives, where it all but dares pastors to give Paul's emphasis its due (Chapter 9).

THEOLOGICAL SCHOOLS

Schools of theology have also contributed to the reticence preachers feel about including grace in sermons by teaching that law and grace must be held in some kind of tension. This tension can be expressed in writing. It can be uttered in words, but in the workplace world, law rules. This does make for tension between people, but not because the grace of God is on their minds. Not only is the good news of personal amnesty obscured by this striving for balance, but it also communicates the notion that law and grace are somehow of equal value. Paul's focus on grace becomes lost in this theological high wire act.

In this book, we shall attempt to show that law and grace are not only qualitatively different, but that because grace is trump, there is no tension to protect and no conditions to announce. The church needs a more grace-filled lectionary engaging the workplace assembled each Sunday. There is no need to wait until the pastor retires.

However, to lift the weight of that lectionary tradition, preachers will need to become aware of the necessity of grace in the workplace (pew space). Generations may come and go before the established authorities officially lift the burden, but weightlifting is the purpose of this book. Even if human nature shows a propensity for living under the law, God does not, and that is what makes grace good news today.

CONVERSATION STARTERS

FOR CHAPTER 1

If you are a preacher, do you do anything to blunt the impact of law-oriented Gospel texts when they appear?

Is the law orientation for Christians limited to Lutherans?

Whether you are a lay-person or a preacher, do you think of the folks lined up on a Sunday morning in the pews as a 'workforce'?

How do you feel about referring to a passage as the "Gospel for the Day" when it is filled with law, admonishment, or the wrath of God?

Two Foundations

2

THE NEWLY APPOINTED CEO, Rene McPherson, entered the room where the Dana Corporation's Board of Directors was assembled for its first meeting with him. He carried a thirteen-inch stack of papers, upon which were printed the regulations governing the company. Included were the structure and function of management, how foremen and superintendents related to employees, and how performance reviews were to be conducted.

His first question was directed to the Chairman of the Board: "Are all of these important to the company?"

"Yes!" came the immediate reply.

"Which ones do you consider most important?" Rene next asked him.

"Oh, I really haven't had time to read them," the Chairman of the Board responded.

"Well," said McPherson, "if you haven't read them they can't be important."

Toting the stack of guidelines to the nearest wastebasket, they became fodder for the dumpster. The Board knew it was getting a CEO with new ideas, but none assumed they would be this radical. Then came the bombshell.

Opening a folder on the table in front of him, Rene distributed one sheet to each member of the Board. They were not surprised at the opening thoughts about profit and growth. What shocked them was the rest of the page. It made the hourly workers the centerpiece, as if on their relationship to each other and to management the rise or fall of the company would depend.[1] Today, Dana, a manufacturer of axles and drive shafts for cars, has 63,000 employees. Needless to say, it rose.

Most corporations still have their stack of guidelines admired by the echelons of power. Thus Dana and the majority rest on two different foundations. Juxtaposed, these principles include the following:

DANA	MOST CORPORATIONS
Eliminate fear and threat that come from performance reviews.	Use fear to motivate accountability
Problems on the floor are solved by small groups of workers at the time they experience them.	Solutions to problems come from the top down.
Groups can make mistakes without threat of reprisals or penalty.	Mistakes are met with the threat of penalty.

The Dana focus did not originate with McPherson. It reflected the thinking circulated for several decades by an American, W. Edwards Deming. Though initially rejected here in the U.S., his ideas found a home in Japan and turned that country around economically after World War II.

The concept, however, did not even originate with Deming. The principles embedded in the ideas of Deming and McPherson, about leaders sharing power and eliminating fear, were first articulated by Jesus and Paul, Inc. in Century One. Jesus was the first leader to inform his followers that they would not "lord it over others," and Paul detailed how unmerited grace trumps law. Whether aware of it or not, Deming and McPherson demonstrated a kinship with this thinking. Where it exists, God is at work. The Creator is neither seen, heard, nor felt, but works subliminally in the weekday workplace as a hidden pressure for social justice. His agenda was originally revealed through writers of Scripture.[2]

Since those at the top are hired to "lord it over others," Deming was on target when he insisted that only CEOs and other top officials should attend his conferences. He believed that for "workplace democracy" to succeed, company officials had to accept the principles. Dana happened because its CEO was squarely behind it.

MOST CORPORATIONS

Relatively few corporations in North America are like Dana, but then neither is the church like Jesus, its Lord. Many leaders in both realms cannot give up the concept of subordination. Accountability is the new standard of law. Deming's ideas made a big splash when first dropped in the corporate pond here, but since then, we have had to be content with ripples.

A reoccurring clue to the present weekday situation happens every semester in my sociology classes. We spend a three-hour session on the North American workplace, and in one of the midterm take-home essay questions students are to show how the ideas of Deming and McPherson would improve the situation where they work or have worked. If their workplace already implements them, the students describe how. In every semester since 1987, students who share how things could be improved outnumber those who are already witnessing their effects, by a ten to one ratio. Bosses who do not seek out the views of employees are a major thorn in the side of rapport.

One student described this in office terms. The CEO's room is large, with a mahogany desk and a wall-to-wall rug. Fear is structured into the furniture. The desk has no blotter on it, and is uncluttered, conveying the impression of a clear minded, well-organized executive with everything under control. Top-down decisions descend from this setting. The desk is not on a raised platform, but like that of a courtroom bench, the effect is still intimidating (and meant to be) for anyone entering the room. A secretary, busy typing just outside the door, schedules appointments. Hourly workers are seldom on her list unless they have been "called on the carpet."

The above illustrations update and affirm unprecedented data obtained by the author, data that includes the church.[3] While employed in a national church research department, a team of laypersons was asked to submit a list of words heard most frequently in the workplace and in church. The top six words from each setting were selected for a question that two hundred laypersons would answer. The larger group included teachers, personal assistants (secretaries), doctors, mechanics, computer programmers, and those in business and sales.

The words that greeted the two hundred respondents were in the following order: competent, accountable, truth, expectations, grace, produce, support, performance, acceptance, justice, achievement, and compassion. We assumed the words would be familiar, since other lay persons had selected them, but we did not know if two distinguishable lists would show up or how often each word was heard—frequently, occasionally, or hardly ever. We did not know if there would be any crossovers—words heard in both realms. When the results were compiled, words from church and work tended to be grouped separately, as shown in the table overleaf. (Only the percents for "frequently" are here, so church and work figures are not to be added together.)

The percentages demonstrate that even with the larger group of respondents, the twelve words had two distinct locations. There was some crossing over but not much. The numerical totals for each word were subjected to three statistical tests—Chi Square, correlation, and T. The results from each test were statistically significant, meaning that they were not by chance or coincidence; there was a valid reason for them. Thus, if the question were put to several million other persons having a Lutheran church and daily work background, the direction of the percentages would be the same. For readers who are familiar with statistics, the Chi Square was off the chart.

	HEARD FREQUENTLY	
	% In Church	%At Work
Grace	96	4
Compassion	87	13
Truth	86	23
Acceptance	61	19
Support	59	35
Justice	48	24
Expectations	7	77
Performance	11	75
Accountable	14	74
Produce	7	71
Competent	8	67
Achievement	13	66

The data suggest that two incompatible linguistic foundations theoretically govern what happens in the workplace and in church. And it should be underscored that Lutherans have no monopoly on the "church words." What we have here are two realms of meaning moving away from each other, lending credence to the cliché that business is business and religion is religion. Moreover, that management is the enforcer is implicit in workplace words. In practice, this is true in church, too.

When a church-place adult forum of laypersons discussed this question in 2004, two of the fifteen felt that "truth" and "acceptance" would crossover more today, due to corporate awareness of CEO corruption and diversity. These were less known in 1980. Thus, if the test were to be repeated today, with the words "diversity" and "harassment" included, they might well be among those heard frequently at work.

ACCOUNTABILITY AND FORGIVENESS

The importance given to the word "accountable" warrants commentary. It would seem to be a counterpart to the importance given to "performance," performance reviews being the method by which accountability is assessed. This implies that intimidation and fear are used as motivation.

Paul uses the word "accountable" in his letter to the Romans (Chapter 3) when addressing the impact of law, but it fades when he proceeds to consider how grace and the righteousness (goodness) of God overshadow the law.

In contrast to the workplace words, the church words reflect a different domain, one that connotes empathy or feeling with someone. Contrasted, they tie in with the observation of John Raines, a Protestant professor at Temple University, who, when speaking at the Third Annual Conference on Religion and Labor, said: "As a nation we are trying to keep two sets of books. One called capital, the other community. One called profits and the other people."[4]

While church and work words reflect two foundations, Dana is much closer to the church than the workplace word list. It also provides an example of God silently at work during the week. It seems reasonable to assert that forgiveness is operational in eliminating the fear in performance reviews and allowing small, on-site quality control groups to make mistakes without reprisal. This is what God specializes in all week long; there is no forgiveness without God and no God without forgiveness.

Ironically, while Dana is in tune with church sources, most congregations are closer to the other workplace foundation, where pastors, bishops, and a pope make the decisions. Thus, the prominence given to the word "grace" in the church list is suspect. While "grace" is indeed present in hymns and liturgical expressions, it is seldom proclaimed in a sermon or applied to life. Although forgiveness was present in some of Jesus' teachings, he never used the word "grace," as noted in Chapter 1.

The above respondents were not asked about the effect of the workplace words on the words heard in church. However, given the top-down structure in which work words function, and the amount of time people spend there, it is not surprising that lay folks have a law orientation to life. Besides, at work, when expectations are not met, company officials can be very unforgiving.

What might at first seem like a subtle difference shows up in the use of language that relates to law and grace. Driving in a city, one can spot "Practice random acts of kindness" on a billboard. The message is nice, but it illustrates the law's disguise. If we are the receivers of such kindness, that act can become unearned grace, something we do not deserve. But as an admonishment the billboard conveys a demand. In relation to God, when we are told God loves us, it's good news, but when we are exhorted to love God it changes into law. As phrases go "the love of God" is ambiguous. Whether it is law or grace depends on whether we interpret it as something we are to do or something God does.

The pulpit has a unique opportunity to speak candidly about law and grace, and to apply it. Then, not only do we hear the word, but it can fertilize the seedling that is faith.

REFLECTIONS

The grace of God had power in the 16th Century because the Reformation exposed the tyranny of law that held sway over the structure and message of the church. The contrast became striking! Today, Christianity has, on this decisive point, lost its basic grasp of grace. That perception is clear and effective only if the accusing law is unveiled at the point where it is accusing us today.[5]

Today, law is accusing us in two places—church and the weekday world. Each mirrors the other. In Chapters 3 and 4 we will show how this happens in church. In this chapter, we are removing the veil from the secular side of these two kingdoms. Only by exposing the tyranny of law in both realms can the contrast of grace become clear, however, and only in clarity does it become meaningful.

Workplace regulations may be moral, amoral, or immoral, but they still function as demands. Indeed, these demands and expectations of daily work can weigh us down. To stay home from work with a clear conscience may take a snowstorm, and even then it might be necessary to have *tried* to get to the work site.

We do live in a meritocracy. In sports, competition has its own bottom line—second place is no place. In college, competition for grades becomes paramount with scholarships going to those who score the highest. A- is still a good grade, but for many college students even a B+ is tainted with failure. C's may be statistically average but the only thing they do for those with eyes on the job market is to undermine self-esteem so necessary for achieving a career goal.

"Grace" may be heard on Sunday, but Monday "merit" prevents its integration into a functional faith for most workers. Grace does not come through as unconditional or unearned, but sounds like something more to do. Sermons need to articulate this discrepancy. Inside the heads of laypersons who sit in the pews on Sunday there is the constant, familiar voice, insisting that they do it 'the old fashioned way'—by earning it. Grace, however, is the proverbial "free lunch," yet so few who are hungry for it, realize this.

The tyranny of work is especially strong today where both parents work, or where one parent has to work two jobs to make the ends meet. Also, those who are subjected to piecework or quotas feel it. Moreover, home is the workplace for many parents. There, too, daytime hours become a race with the clock, keeping the house, sorting the wash, chauffeuring offspring to lessons and medical appointments, shopping for groceries, and then getting home in time to put supper on the table. And this does not include the time it takes to think up the daily menu or ponder what clothing to buy for fast-growing children. Life has "must do" written all over it. Time off is scarce. These demands may or may not have a moral attachment, but they help condition mind and conscience. The Author of Life seems like a taskmaster who demands perpetual responsibility in and outside the church building.

Ironically, the church played a significant part to the moral side of this tyranny. Both John Calvin and Martin Luther unwittingly made contributions to it in the Reformation. Through Calvin and the Puritan work ethic came the belief that sloth was a deadly sin, whereas the capacity to work hard was taken as a sign that such a worker had already received divine grace. From Luther came the concept of "callings," and while he sought to dignify all work with that distinction, a by-product was the belief that if we slack off, we are failing to be good stewards. Thus, we have two employers: one who is almighty and one who is finite, but either one can ruin our whole day. As Max Weber puts it, "In the Reformation one thing was unquestionably new. The fulfillment of one's duty in daily work was the highest form of moral activity the individual could assume."[6] Daily work took on a religious significance, but it was steeped in law.

There is biblical support for the effect of the workplace lifted up in this chapter. In Jesus' Parable of the Talents, profit making, performance, and accountability receive strong sanction. The reader may recall how in Matthew 25, a "master" gives three servants varying amounts of money to be used wisely. The one who received the most money came through well, as did the next in line. However, the one who received the least was severely reprimanded for not turning a profit. He was expected to compete with the five-talent (money amount) people, but he failed.

Despite this being a parable of Jesus, if we modernize the story we confront a critical issue. We might liken the Creator to a card dealer who gives each of us a hand to play. If the Dealer deals the cards by chance, what we have is analogous to a genetic lottery. Either way, however, what happens next is our move, which many would call free will, but here is the crux of the issue. If one has five trump cards, that player can do well. On the other hand, if a player has only one trump card, like the single-talent man in Jesus' parable, or the poor, the game is not exactly encouraging. The odds are not in his or her favor. A single trump card is not enough. The bottom line? In life, choices depend upon one's hand.

Whether our hand is by divine design or by luck, we have a way of understanding why some people answer opportunity's knock and why others do not make it to the door. If the Creator bestows more "blessings" on some folks than on others, the reason we are not all created equal boils down to preferential treatment for those already ahead (tax breaks for the wealthy), a reality hard to reconcile with Jesus' other parable, the one about the Generous Employer who, at the end of the day, paid all the same, regardless of when they started to work.

CONVERSATION STARTERS

FOR CHAPTER 2

Would any of the Dana guidelines improve things where you work? If so, which ones?

Why does a secular duty still place a demand on the conscience?

What does "working hard for a free lunch" mean to you?

Is it fair to expect a one-talent person at work or school to compete with the five or even three-talent persons? Why or why not?

"In his often-provocative book, Paul G. Johnson considers grace, the theological basis of the Lutheran understanding of God and the workplace, the place where most people spend a significant part of their lives. He challenges Christians in general, and clergy in particular, to rediscover the central place that a theology of grace should occupy in our faith. In so doing, he issues an important challenge to the current use (in his opinion overuse) of Dietrich Bonhoeffer's concept of 'cheap grace' by insisting this passing reference has been blown out of all proportion to make a contemporary understanding of grace a thinly disguised return to the law. He also challenges the wider church to rethink their current lectionary selections that he believes places far too much emphasis on the law side of the law Gospel dialectic. These are serious challenges and the author offers compelling arguments to rethink our current lack of a grace-centered theology. In raising these questions, his book is intrinsically an important one.

The second large area of consideration is the place of grace in the workplace. Johnson correctly points to the silence of preaching and spiritual direction in this vital area. He offers some intriguing parables of workplace theology and encourages us to mature of our spiritual understanding as we consider how the love of God can operate in an increasingly secular world. In so doing, he is attempting to reestablish God's love in a place where most of us spend a majority of our waking hours. It is an ambitious start and one that should result in much fruitful dialogue."

Alfred C. Acer, Pastor, Reformation Lutheran Church, West Long Branch, New Jersey

3

SOON AFTER LEAVING MY first parish, I began reflecting on what happened there. For the first three years, I preached on Sunday in an established church building, but in the fourth year we started a new mission in a town beyond the service area of the congregation. In the new setting we first met in homes, early church style, and it was a breath of fresh air. We sat in living rooms and everybody talked about the biblical text for that Sunday, giving rise to a variety of interpretations.

In the older, established church, one person delivered the sermons— me. I typed them out then, and after four years a tally revealed that over 800,000 words had been spoken from the pulpit. Week after week it was the same voice in twenty-minute segments. There were no breaks; words were non-stop, coming from altar, pulpit, choir loft and pews, spoken or sung. The church was a mouth house.

Gradually, it dawned on me that no matter what I said in the sermon, when the service ended, the only words to me from the parishioners as they walked by at the door, or stood around having a cup of coffee, were "Good morning Pastor." No one said a word about the sermon that I had spent hours preparing and twenty minutes delivering. Judging from the post-worship conversation, you would never have known people had been within earshot of the Word just a few minutes before.

I recall the Fiftieth Anniversary celebration of another congregation. The guest preacher, Dean of Harvard's Divinity School, had just delivered a stimulating message. However, when we moved to the parish hall for "high tea," no one mentioned the sermon. Smalltalk shaped the conversation: work being done on the church grounds, the Boston Red Sox, or an incident during the week at work. It was as if the sermon were a sacred cow to be observed, not digested.

A little solace is found in the experience of a famous preacher from the 4th Century, John Chrysostom, referred to as the "Golden Mouth." Indeed, the people of Greece not only listened to him, but also responded to his sermons with applause, and not just when he said "Amen." This custom, common in the circus and theater, followed folks right into church. So ingrained was this practice, a preacher reddened with shame if the end of his sermon was met with silence.[1]

Though at first Chrysostom found "very human pleasure" in this response, it began to weigh on him that maybe the congregation's reaction was a fleeting one, especially when in competition with chariot racing, pew sitting placed second or third. What really bothered this pulpiteer from antiquity was how people praised his preaching, but could not offer feedback on anything he said, even in their own words.[2] That their posture of only listening created a moat between their thoughts and their words never occurred to him. He assumed, perhaps erroneously, that those who applauded "received no benefits at all" from his words. One Sunday, he suggested that instead of applause people ponder the content of the message and discuss it at home with their families.[3] The assembled church erupted into the sound of many hands clapping.

If his "fans" marveled at his words, Chrysostom may have wondered how they could so easily forsake the Word for the horses. We also do not know if he considered that the applause was in response to his making contact with their thought processes. Today, it can trouble a pastor why the "summers" seem to be getting longer. Folks used to come back right after Labor Day. Now, the vacation can extend into October. Why, if the Word occurs?

Nevertheless, words of unmerited grace can heal, if we take a fresh look at our delivery system and prepare accordingly. To that end, Chrysostom beckons us.

WHAT HAPPENS TO THE SERMON

This may not be a question for preachers who assume God is at work making all the relevant contact. This assumption, however, helps dictate the "no comment" response; the pulpit stands six feet above contradiction. In some churches it is higher, but even if the sermon is delivered on the floor of the nave, no one from the pews dares break the sound barrier. One pastor planted a question in the choir. At a designated spot in the sermon a young man stood up and said, "Pastor, I don't agree with you." Most folks were so shocked, they did not hear what he had to say. Why this silence persists on the way out of church or in the parish hall is something else.

In part, silence is due to the unintended intimidation of the setting. Surrounded by holy furniture—altar, pulpit, pews, organ, choir loft, and baptismal font—there exudes a sacred aura. What the preacher wears adds to the ambience. And then there are the years spent studying theology and the Bible. Some preachers believe the sermon is the Word of God or a means of grace. For Anglican Martin Lloyd-Jones, the pulpit is not only God's method, but God's "only method" of communicating the Word.[4] What happens to it once it leaves the preacher is of no concern to him; the sermon occurs in the pulpit where words are raised to the highest power.

Dietrich Ritschl of Austin Presbyterian Seminary shies away from homiletical transubstantiation, since he believes the words are his. However, he also believes that God enters them once they are airborne, enabling them to make a relevant landing in the minds of those grounded in the pews.[5] For centuries, preachers have labored, often on Saturday night, under the assumption that God would be there in the morning, somehow speaking through them and bringing the message to bear efficaciously upon the thoughts of the faithful. Besides, God promises: "My word will not return void," and standing before rows of silent people, that is somewhat reassuring.

Nevertheless, there are several fallacies in the above theological assumptions. One is that the listener can receive in twenty minutes what it took the preacher hours to prepare. Although what is delivered is not the labor pain, but the baby, it is no secret, at least to the preacher, that much thought is given to what to say. What to preach on, what the text says, how it relates to today, are questions that ignite clergy cognition. And what may be foreign to the people is the extent to which the pastor searches for the interpretation of a passage or parable that is most palatable to him-herself. Preachers have a choice. Listeners do not.

A second fallacy is closely linked to the first. To deliver a twenty-minute homily, it is considered necessary to spend three years in a religious think tank, a theological school where raising questions, discussing issues, and articulating one's thoughts is the daily diet. Much time is spent in reading and taking notes, while listening to lectures. Then, as the semester winds down, this dialogue turns to the computer, where term papers are churned out.

There is good reason for this multi-dimensional approach to learning. In 1956, an educational board of a national church published a four-part pie chart. It showed that we retain 90 percent of what we learn by doing, 75 percent of what we speak, 50 percent of what we read, and only 10 percent from listening.[6]

We have been expecting to get from listening to one person talk what preachers themselves could only receive through the combined cognitive-linguistic mediums of listening, reading, speaking, and writing. We have taken the gospel content with us into the parish, but left the assimilation process back in the seminary.

That something so obvious could be missed is not surprising. Anything done the same way, over and over, hardens into a tradition that obscures assessment. It becomes an unwritten norm, in this case, one that says preachers can think for people. What reality declares is that thinking is non-transferable.

Data supports the 10 percent figure. A lecturer can cruise along at a speaking rate of 100 words per minutes, but the listener can take in up to 700 words per minute. We think much faster than we speak. When the mind is engaged in audible expression, it slows to a crawl.

Listening to a sermon, therefore, is like traveling fifteen mph in a sixty-five mph zone. And since we have too much mind time, we may just take off on our own up a side street and park there. Putting it another way, we are constantly "talking" within ourselves; it is impossible to keep our minds blank even for a second.

When the words leave the mouth of the preacher and reach the outer ear of the listener, they do so as sound waves—not words—which strike the eardrum and travel as impulses to the central nervous system. There, two actions occur almost simultaneously. First, a preliminary selection is made by part of the brain on *what* to focus attention. If chosen for further consideration, the word triggers a search for *where* in the memory it fits. While pew sitters are not conscious of these actions, the reason a person may mentally wander off during a sermon is that the brain does not come up with a match often enough to keep the mind tuned in.

The time it takes to make the selection and finish the search for a word or idea may be no more than one-fifth of a second. Thus, much that leaves the mouth of a speaker decays within two seconds of reaching the listener's ear. Impulses that survive reach what is called the "short-term memory system," where the process of selective attention continues. Much of what gets this far—sentences and trains of thought—decays within thirty seconds.[7] Since we don't take notes, we cannot bring it to mind after the service ends. Impulses that come from a story or illustration may linger because interest has been aroused. The context, however, is not absorbed, and the listener does not grow in understanding; in effect, we experience something akin to sacred entertainment.

The sermon is in the church, but the listener's mind is in the weekday world. It tunes in if some connection is made. Pew sitters can attend for months without ever hearing a reference or illustration that pertains to where they devote the best hours and years of their lives—daily work. In fairness, it is difficult for a preacher to make the average midweek workplace relevant, since he or she does not spend much time there, and those who left that background to attend a seminary are prone to forget or 'put aside' such roots.

Colleges and universities have known, since 1953, that students are more active mentally during a discussion than in just listening to a lecture.[8] Although many professors engage students in dialogue, especially in the social sciences, when it comes to the pulpit/pew setting in church, "lecturing" is the mode of speech. Presumably, the assumption that God is active in church but not in a classroom has prevented theological schools from taking such "secular" data seriously.

THE BELL RINGER

Mindful of the ten percent figure, and not ready to believe the minds in the pews were blanks, in a subsequent parish, I resolved to do a little research on my own. Having obtained the consent of the church council to conduct an experiment, it was announced one Sunday in September that at some time that Fall a bell would ring during a sermon, at which time everyone would have the opportunity to jot down whatever was going on in their minds at that moment.[9] It was announced this way, with sufficient explanation, so that when it did happen, no explanation would be needed, and the chance for distraction would be minimized. Since it would happen when the congregation least expected it, their written words would reflect a candid exposure of their actual thoughts. At first, people sat on the mental edge of the pews in anticipation, but as the weeks went by and the bell did not ring, they mentally settled back for the sermonic offering.

Three months later, when the bell sounded, it caught everyone by surprise. For a second they all just sat there. Then, throughout the church, folks reached for pieces of paper placed in the back of each hymnal and began writing. Categorizing the results revealed both active and passive cerebral activity. Eight kinds of active thoughts were identifiable. These included questions raised and answered (in the minds of listeners), questions raised but left unanswered, dissent, personal experiences related to the sermon content, personal conflict, personal conviction, implications drawn, and conclusions reached. Sixty percent had these active thoughts, whereas forty percent had what we called "passive thoughts." They wrote down what they had just heard me say, but no more.

The category "questions raised but not answered" warrants an immediate observation. Early in the 5th Century, Augustine was known to solicit questions from people present in a Mass so that none would misunderstand what he was saying, and in his writing on styles of preaching he explicitly advocates this practice. His words are worth noting:

> It is exceedingly desirable that whatever occurs to the mind as an objection [question] . . . should be stated, lest it turn up at a time when no one will be there to answer it, or if it should occur to one who is present but says nothing about it, it might never be thoroughly resolved.[10]

INCREASING THE MILEAGE

In this book the good news of grace transcends the law orientation of daily work and the Bible. Allowing unearned grace to enter means lifting the veil on the way both daily work and biblical law accuse us. The tyranny of the law today has a double edge, in contrast to the time of the Reformation, when it was mainly ecclesiastical. By revealing both edges, their power can be reduced, and grace more appreciated.

For purposes of awareness, any pastor and congregation could replicate the above bell-ringing experiment, and publish the results in a church newsletter or a special pulpit/pew handout. It could be explained as a way of ascertaining what form thinking takes in the pews during a sermon. That it does not make it to the door or the coffee hour should be shared also, even though laypersons already know that. What laypersons (and perhaps clergy) do not know is why. What they will also not be aware of is that many of those sitting in the pews are giving thought to what is being said from the pulpit during the sermon. It would provide incentive to talk to someone in church—about the sermon.

If this experiment is tried, it must be remembered that the results do not relate to the size of a parish or to the sermon; the content of the message is not being evaluated but the mode of communication. The issue here is not the message or the messenger, but the ten percent medium. The power of a preacher to hold an audience is not questioned, nor is the fact that some speakers are better than others. What is at stake is the inability of the sermon to do more than capture attention and hold interest. The church-building structure and worship format do not allow people to reflect on, and thus assimilate, the meaning of the words. This is a universal incongruity. It is no one's fault; it's just the way it is, and has been for a long time.

Since most conversations commence with a question being raised, a basic one in this context would be "did the sermon prompt any questions for you this morning?" Obviously, the pastor can encourage this by suggesting it be asked, and to augment the process pew sitters might also be invited to jot down a question that comes to mind during the sermon. Doing that would automatically increase the retention percentage from ten to seventy-five percent on at least one point.

Another way the preacher can encourage response is to pose a couple of different interpretations to something in a text and invite worshippers to share which one is more meaningful and why. These reactions could also become part of the coffee hour conversation, or be talked over elsewhere with someone who heard the sermon.

In relation to the content of this book, the subject area wherein the preacher can be most helpful is that time-consuming experience known as weekday work. Chapter 2 provided information for entering this world, but at this point it should be noted that hearing this from the pulpit, in a way that reflects the workplace standards and expectations weighing on the minds of worshipers, would do two things. One, it would establish a connection between pulpit and pew, based on reality. Since the workplace is so much a part of the lives of pew sitters, to hear a sermon relating to it cannot help but increase the attention level given to the sermon. And the other: it would say to the listener that the preacher is trying to understand where the pew sitters spend most of their time. It is like tying in to a mindset.

It may be news to most persons to learn about the weekday preconceptions that accompany them to worship. When the tyranny or weight of the law, sacred or secular, is revealed, the mind can begin to realize that grace contains something vital for faith, indeed, lies at the heart of it.

In congregations where small groups provide a source of communication, the law and grace content of this book can be food for thought. This is also true of the sermon itself. The sermon can be the beginning of a communication process, not the end of it. It need not stop with the Amen, and it need not be followed with silence.

If there are no small group conversation opportunities, there is a precedent for providing one. It was a primary means of communication for Jesus. On occasion he spoke to large groups but everyday he was with twelve people. Of logistical necessity they were men, but that restriction no longer applies. This takes seriously the means of communication that emerged when the first Christians met in homes. The starting place would be the existing pulpit/pew experience, but that could allow an appetite for small group conversation to develop.

One subject to consider would be ways in which both law and grace are experienced where people work. In this way, the group could provide the weekday application for the sermon, making it a part of the Word for the day.

CONVERSATION STARTERS

FOR CHAPTER 3

Try to recall a story you heard in a sermon and share it with someone.

If the effect of sermons is so minimal, why has it continued as a mode of communication for so long?

Why might preachers not relate to the present day in their sermons?

Why would a sermon that relates to the workplace put people mentally on the edge of the pews?

Was Jesus' initial small group of twelve intentional or coincidental?

HOLDING LAY FEET TO THE FIRE

4

WALK INTO A BANK, any bank. At first what speaks is security. Cameras follow your every move. Tellers are easily spotted behind glass barriers or barred windows. Privacy partitions greet the public, but what the public does not see or interpret, a teller attending one of my sociology classes did.

From the front, she described, all tellers appear to be created equal. Even behind customer windows nothing is between the tellers but mini-counters. Every two tellers share this inside counter space. As a worker moves up in the ranks, separations become more apparent. The head teller has her own counter and does not have to share her printer or workspace. This small piece of privacy is a status symbol; the more separate space, the more prestige, and vice versa.

Should one graduate to customer service, she is removed from the teller line and provided an office area. The branch manager has a closable door to his/her office, giving them still more prestige. The Vice President of Security also has an office on the first floor, but separated from the Customer Service offices, it gives him more status and privacy. Upstairs is where the top management people are. To work there is to move up, literally and symbolically. Additional chains of command and divisions are provided 'up there', making for an overlapping bureaucracy.

The reader may recall a student's description of the CEO's office in a different corporation identified in Chapter 2. It featured one room with a rug, a large cleared off desk, a davenport along one wall, and a personal secretary next door who arranged appointments and typed letters. The furniture spoke of status and income levels.

THE CHURCH AS MODEL

Mindful of the propensity for human nature to *lord* it over others and the effect this has on everyone, Jesus said to his disciples, "It shall not be so among you" (Matthew 20:25-27).

Jesus, no doubt, had reasons for this guideline. We know that stress comes from the aura of authority. Because few egos can handle the self-importance it creates, it leads to officiousness, and even a suggestion from such a source can come across as a command. Yet today, if someone mentions this, he or she is said to have an "authority complex." In reality, it is the officious one who has the complex.

In an effort to prevent this development, however, Jesus inaugurated a lay movement. He selected a small group of males to provide a nucleus, but none of them attended a theological school or were ordained. They did have a three-year training period, but they all flunked. Assuming that Jesus intentionally bypassed the religious powers in favor of laypersons, his admission standards were rather low. It was a new idea in religion, designed to spread authority horizontally, not vertically.

A second guideline on leadership in the Gospels explicitly states, "Call no man master, father, or rabbi, for there is but one master and one Father, and all of you are brothers and sisters" (Matthew 23:8). Some question whether Jesus said these words since calling a priest "father" came later. However, even if the words were added, their importance stands. It means that for a while the authority invested in titles and the structure implicit in "pedestals" were not believed to be in keeping with the spirit of Christ. True to that spirit, the first twelve male recruits had no titles.

From Jesus' words it seems legitimate to conclude that religious titles are honorary degrees ecclesiastical authorities bestow upon themselves. There is no way a person with Jesus' awareness would be a willing party to a hierarchy in his own house. However, authoritarianism can emerge anywhere, including banks.

Were Jesus to return today in a visible form what might he say about the direction his church took? This is the incentive for a book by retired Roman Catholic priest, Joseph Girzone. Living on the edge of a town in western Pennsylvania, as a wood carver by the name of Joshua, people do not recognize the character of Jesus, but what he says and does remind them of someone. His candid words prompts one of them to ask what he thinks about religion.

He tells them frankly that church religion has become a structure super-imposed on people.[1] When a Catholic asks him what he thinks of their pastor, Joshua observes, to the dismay of some, that he is not a bad person, but he puts the law first, people second.[2] He adds that it is hard to enjoy being God's children in the presence of an authority that needs to be in control.

This not only gets Joshua in trouble with the pastor, but also, an audience with the pope. Standing before the pontiff, a Swiss Guard tells him to kneel before his holiness and kiss his ring, neither of which Joshua does. He also reminds the pope (who does not know this is Jesus) that Jesus named twelve apostles not just one (there were others named and unnamed in the Gospels). Joshua informs the pope that people are drawn to God through humility, whereas adulation for a man settles on that man alone.[3]

It is reasonable to assume that the existence of hierarchies in Christendom reveals the inability of various believers in Jesus to follow him at that point. We see an extreme example of this in Matthew. He records how Jesus gave Peter the "keys of the kingdom," which meant that Peter would decide who would be forgiven and who would not (Matthew 16:19-20). It is hard to imagine a leader who frowned on human beings lording it over others, allowing the eternal destiny of anyone to be based on the say so of a group of men (or women), let alone on one.

Evidence that early Christians did take these teachings of Jesus seriously is present in what the Bible tells of that period. When his Jerusalem followers sold their property and pooled their resources in order to meet the needs of the poor, it suggested oneness. In Asia Minor, early Christians met in homes without ordained clergy. There were worship leaders, but maleness would not have been a prerequisite. Jesus' criticism of Martha for staying in the kitchen would not have been lost on female hostesses of home meetings (Luke 10:38-42). The home was a good place for leadership to cross gender lines. In 110 CE, when Ignatius of Antioch sought to consolidate the house churches around the concept of a bishop, the role of women began to recede and the male hijacking of the church began.[4]

Inasmuch as a number of these fledgling congregations or house churches were organized by Paul with his strong emphasis on grace, there was an added reason to stay within the parameters of a lay movement set forth by Jesus. A grace orientation needs no chain of command. Since grace is a free gift, it can only be extended, or offered. It is with law enforcement that a chain of command develops.

And develop it did, relegating Paul's distinction between law and grace to the Latin Bible, where it sat for centuries. Nestled in its pages and waiting to be discovered, however, was the dispute between Peter and Paul on the issue of law. Peter wanted the Jewish law to be included when Jews or Gentiles became Christians, but Paul reached the point in Ephesians (2:14-16), where he declared that Christ "abolished the law, with its commandments [the Big Ten] and ordinances," and created one humanity in relation to himself, free of gender, race, or class distinctions. He removed the wall of hostility erected by the law. Paul understandably believed unmerited grace altered the emphasis on law for everyone, as it had for him.

That a priesthood emerged favoring law is ironic since the location was Rome. Not only did Paul have a vested interest in a congregation there, he also sent a theological letter on the difference between law and grace to that congregation. Indeed, that Peter and not Paul was named the first pope suggests leaders in Rome *preferred* law to grace.[5] They would have been aware of Peter's and Paul's views on law, and which one's views would be more compatible with their control orientation.

LUTHER'S LEGACY ON LAW

When we switch the spotlight to the Protestant Reformation figure, Martin Luther, we discover how walls unwittingly continued, even though it was thought they had been removed. These walls talk now.

The common assumption is that the basis of Luther's' faith was the Pauline principle of justification by grace. However, this hides the place law had in Luther's mind. In his Commentary on Galatians he wrote: "To divide Law and Gospel means to place the Gospel in heaven, and to keep the Law on earth." In relation to society, "obedience to the Law is severely required. In civil life Gospel, grace, forgiveness of sins and Christ himself, do not count, but only Moses and the law-books."[6] This led to his notion of two kingdoms. Through the state (one kingdom) the left hand of God literally executes law-breakers, whereas through the church (the other kingdom), the right hand of forgiveness is dispensed in Word and Sacrament.

Thus, civil powers had it both ways. They found in the concept of two kingdoms both salvation for their own souls and an excuse to maintain society's status quo. The very injustice in the world that might impose a sense of guilt upon their conscience was maintained when Luther located the gospel in heaven and the law on earth.

With grace removed from a weekday habitat, the letter of the law and divine wrath ruled this world. In 1525, German peasants took the Gospel to mean that God would not want them mired in misery. When they sought to negotiate their grievances with the civil authorities, Luther privately supported them. But, when the peasants rebelled, Luther publicly came down on the side of law and order. His two-kingdom theory gave ecclesiastical sanction to the slaughter of the peasants, a number that reached 100,000. Social and economic justice was not an issue then, Indulgences were.

Perhaps Luther's aim was to keep grace pure and unfettered. After all, grace alone had liberated him from his futile efforts to please God by flagellation and penitence. The importance he placed on law is seen, however, in his *Small Catechism* (which non-Lutherans also use). A staple in confirmation courses, it calls for ten sessions on the Commandments—law—and one session on the Second Article of the Apostle's Creed—gospel. The word "grace" appears three times in the *Small Catechism* but is never explained. At the end of the Commandments, grace is promised to all who keep them, but Luther's own experience was the reverse. Little wonder that in 1990 the Search Institute in Minneapolis found that 84 percent of active Lutheran youth do not understand grace. Martin's law had their feet firmly in the fire. Ecclesiastical child abuse some might call it.

What is still with us is the effect of Luther's concept of two kingdoms on our perceptions. God has a split personality, from which Jesus is the Savior. Fortunately, God's relationship to Jesus does not *have* to be seen that way (Chapter 6). Moreover, a universal sense of *ought* is built into creation. All cultures frown on stealing and peacetime killing. In a sense, we do not break God's laws anymore than we break the law of gravity by stumbling down the stairs. Falls in either area only prove the laws exist, and that God sustains them. However, not even a fall on the stairs proves divine punishment. The ire of God can be seen as a projection of human wrath, elevating one of humanity's most insidious traits (getting even) to the highest power.

One of the unintended side effects of Luther's thought is to make grace too good to be true. With law dominating this life, grace becomes a kind of fringe benefit. Sheltered from the real world, it is viewed as an experience received after this life has come to a close. Until then, we live our lives under the demands of time and our view of the Creator. In this life we have the redemptive *promise* of God, which enters our awareness through faith, but that's it. Even Luther's perception of Word and Sacrament as a Means of Grace is appropriated by "faith alone." Thus, the actual experience of spiritual fulfillment is deferred until our permanent retirement.

Luther's translation of the Bible into the vernacular made its contents more accessible to the clergy and theological students, but a spin-off from this is still with us. The better versed the clergy grow in the Bible and theology, the further removed from the laity they can become. Earning a living leaves little time and less energy for the laity to read, let alone study theology. On Sunday, when these two kingdoms assemble in church, the separation is accentuated in most churches by what each wears; clergy are set apart by collar and title.

Although Luther believed that everyone was a priest by baptism, and that what an ordained priest does at the altar does not influence God, in effect what he did was to relocate the Word thirty feet closer to the pews. For Protestants, clergy authority has continued—in the pulpit. And as we demonstrated in Chapters 2 and 3, even when grace is proclaimed it is rarely assimilated because most laypersons arrive with a predisposition for law, their feet having been held to the fire all week. Moreover, sermon texts that feature grace show up in the summer when many folks are on vacation. In the interests of "rightly dividing the word of truth," preachers may, on occasion, bring the good news of unmerited grace into a sermon, but it is like a "PS" at the end. Thus, today, when a layperson wishes to become a pastor, he or she must attend a seminary, and then be examined to see if he or she is qualified to think out loud. The implication is clear. Few come to an understanding of grace by just sitting in pews and listening or by attending confirmation classes.

While Luther's experience was but a momentary glimpse of the sun poking through the clouds, his source of inspiration, Paul, will always stand as a biblical witness to the power of grace over law.

IMPACT ON THE WORKFORCE

In most Protestant denominations, congregations have a measure of autonomy. However, should an issue emerge on which they have ecclesiastical laws, then the hierarchical organizational chart comes alive. Letters from bishops are sent to the clergy reminding them of the need for company loyalty. When persons who were once caring and egalitarian become bishops, they suddenly value law first and people second; even unjust laws take on importance. Moral judgment raises its head and the well-known words of Jesus to "judge not" joins grace on the sidelines. Ironically, the observation of Paul can be heard, "You who desire to be under the law, do you not hear the law?" It pressures. It triggers rebellion. It produces guilt feelings, and it holds lay feet to the fire.

But the feet of the laity are already being held to the fire. Such is the purpose of performance reviews. At times, this aptly describes a sermon that follows one of the law-oriented Gospel texts, but sermons pale in comparison to the periodic evaluations to which workforce personnel are subjected. It can be one of the more terrifying experiences a worker has to go through, not least of all because it is always from the top down. Those below do not have the same opportunity to evaluate the boss, foreman, or supervisor. At stake can be a person's job or a raise. While lay-offs and demotions carry their own brands of fear, these can be tied to the outcome of a performance review. CEOs who deploy these measures assume they motivate greater effort and efficiency, but I recall such experiences in a church bureaucracy that tried to model itself after the Hayes Associates, a company that specialized in workplace accountability. It took two weeks after the review to fully concentrate on work. We each had to write up the review and then compare what we had written with what the department head had written.

The secular hierarchical managerial approach also cultivates guilt feelings, some real some false, but both depressing. Retired people who have spent years in the workforce can find that they cannot rest during daytime, without feeling they should be up and about. And if it is a question of staying home for a day, the best way is for it to be the result of snow that prevents getting out of one's driveway. Snow leaves one's conscience free and clear. Law never takes a day off. The only caveats to the snowstorm are that for those who plow snow, it is a source of income, and if teachers in public schools get a snow day, they have to make it up at the end of the school year!

On a more serious note, if a snooze after lunch is taboo, the thought of unemployment devastates those conditioned by the work ethic to regard paid work as the chief reason for getting up in the morning. If one believes that hard work brings rewards and that God has given people special talents for achieving them, then for such a "believer" to have the employment rug pulled away is an assault on faith.

A pastor in Michigan pointed to this when he spoke of church members who lose their jobs also losing their interest in church. Instead of being drawn to the church in a time of need, they were repelled. He said, "If you have been indoctrinated to believe that if you work hard God will take care of you, then when unemployment strikes you begin to wonder what you did to deserve it." [7]

The work ethic is unable to distinguish reasons for unemployment. Whether lay-offs are due to the effect of foreign imports on domestic markets, automation, or outsourcing, tyranny over the mind continues to be nurtured by the hierarchical managerial approach. Medical research has found a link between the suicide rate and the rise in unemployment. Studies in Britain and North America found that 25-50 percent of men were out of work at the time they took their lives. [8]

The impact of hierarchical relationships on people in a workplace setting was poignantly brought home to me while in a hospital, waiting for a procedure known as a barium enema. If you've never had one, you should, it will make your day. I was brought in a wheel chair to the lab. Wearing one of those tie-in-the-back smocks, I lay on the cold metal surface of the lab table. Finally, the door opened and a nurse stepped in. "Mr. Johnson," she announced, "this is Dr. Smith. He will perform the enema for you today." He entered and I waited for him to introduce her. He didn't. I thought, "Doesn't she have a name?" She did, on her uniform, but I had to crane my neck to see it. It was basically an injustice imposed on the nurse.

Both the church and the workplace are under law, until the grace of God intervenes. When it does, the amount of caring and equality increases exponentially. Fortunately, there are individual corporations, both secular and sacred, leading the way in this regard.

CONVERSATION STARTERS

FOR CHAPTER 4

Why have Jesus' guidelines for discipleship quoted in this chapter not become a part of the church?

What difference would placing people ahead of the law make in organized religion?

How did the concept of two kingdoms contribute to the gap between Sunday and Monday or the focus on accountability in church and workplace?

With Paul placing so much emphasis on unmerited grace for this life, how could Martin Luther consign grace to heaven and law to this world?

Do workers consciously accept subordinate positions without the effects described in this chapter?

Can you identify with the freedom that comes from a snowstorm that prevents one from getting to work?

A Memo to the CEO

5

IT WAS NOTED IN the Prologue how you appreciated the group of workers in the lunchroom. You did not know them, but you knew even less about the meaning or context of the word "grace" that had appeared in the note someone had placed on your desk, a note that simply said, "Let grace enter your workplace." "Grace" was not capitalized, so you assumed it was not the name of a person.

When you left the group, grace had entered the workplace, but you didn't realize it. Rare were the times when you actually listened to your workers. At a Board of Directors meetings you looked at those around you. They were all men. You gave the impression of listening to them, but you knew what you wanted to do before the meeting began. You had already decided.

Apparently, you really listened to the lunchroom group because you had no idea what the grace note meant, but you were curious for some reason. Most employees worked "for" you, but after listening to the folks at the lunchroom table you felt you were actually working "with" them to solve a puzzle. You asked them questions, and cared about their answers. Of course, in a sense you were trapped. You sat at a round table. You were but one of a group. Since the table had no corners, it was not conducive to delivering pronouncements. Further thoughts on grace are now in order.

IT BEGINS AT THE TOP

You may recall the name W. Edwards Deming. Forty years ago, he drew the attention of some CEOs, and the ire of others, by advocating what he called "democracy in the workplace." One might think this would be a given in a country that likes to think of itself as a democracy, as we do in America, but despite that ideal, there are pockets of activity within our borders that do not operate that way. For Deming, one of them was the way corporations did business, the way management and labor related to each other as adversaries. Out of his emphasis, and the response to it, came such books as *The Passion for Excellence* by Peters and Austin, and *Reinventing the Corporation* by Naisbitt and Aburdene.

Although his ideas were at first rejected here in the States, they were well received in Japan, and for the economic success they brought to that country, Deming was given a second look here at home. He was in his eighties when he died, but at that time another person—Robert Greenleaf—much younger, was tuning in to the same wavelength. His ideas have been articulated in a number of books advancing the concept of servant leadership.

Greenleaf was moved by the example of Jesus who, though a leader, once stooped so low as to wash the feet of his followers. Although Greenleaf believed that a leader should be a servant of his people, he also felt that a different person should serve as the manager and run the business, leaving the top CEO to develop the servant character of the company. He believed that prayer should guide the CEO, and at that point there was a brand of Christian piety that came through his approach to grace in the workplace.

The term "grace" that appears in the title of this book is a biblically-oriented word. You may not have heard of it much, but that is not really your fault. It's not anyone's fault because it does not appear in the Bible very often. At times it is there implicitly, as we shall have occasion to consider, but its nature and content are fascinating. Once it has entered human thought, it has a power all its own.

To borrow a playing-card term, grace is trump. Law and fear are much more extensive in the Bible and in most literature that claims to be biblically based, but they are like the other thirty-nine cards in the deck. In the game of Contract Bridge, when one suit is declared trump, even a deuce in that suit has the authority to take a trick containing kings, queens, and aces, as you may know.

It is the nature of grace that does this, and like yeast it can give a corporation a lift. It is not the quantity of grace but the quality that lends weight to the word.

The importance of grace became evident to me in a nearby corporation I visited because I had heard that it was a proponent of Deming's "workplace democracy." I thought it would be helpful to interview the CEO, so I called and made an appointment. Shortly after being ushered into his spacious office, he told me how committed they were to Deming's concept. In fact, their motto was "Do it right the first time." Those words seemed to be everywhere, above drinking fountains, in restrooms, and on doors.

Actually, this was not one of Deming's ideas. Over seven hundred corporations have adopted or adapted his philosophy; many have taken what they want and no more. "Do it right the first time" is a focus on law, not grace. It animates neither workplace democracy nor servant leadership. It serves notice to people that they have one shot, and it better hit the target. There is an implicit threat in the motto. It augments fear.

Deming's idea was that workers are more motivated if fear is removed, and thus it was a cardinal tenet of his that after giving small groups of workers the authority to make various kinds of decisions, there should be no reprisal if a group makes a mistake. In religious terms this was grace at work, or forgiveness.

Equally important to Deming was the principle that for this to happen, it has to begin at the top. So adamant was he about this that he only encouraged CEOs and their closest associates to attend his seminars. They came knowing something of his philosophy in advance, but sitting with Deming in a room and listening to this deep-voiced octogenarian turn their views on management upside-down was a shock.

Servant leadership may be more understood because democracy in the workplace has paved the way. Grace benefits from both sources. Why it is seldom heard about is a key part of this book. Workplace democracy tends to have a secular ring to it, while servant leadership is closer to home for the preacher. Grace, on the other hand, is already at "home," but in a closet. It lines the minds of pulpit trainees and pastors who have been trying for years to communicate from the pulpit without it.

Some clergy may respond that grace has no means of entering the workplace. To go anywhere, grace has to have a launching pad, and that's what the church can be. It is the means, or contains the means of grace—Word and Sacraments. What they forget is that the Word joins pulpit and pew. When those in the pews hear thoughts on a subject that genuinely interests them, they can take those thoughts into the workplace. It can then become Monday morning incentive.

THEOLOGY 101

Along with underscoring the value of grace, the other reason for this memo is to let you in on a little secret. When you sit in your office and ponder how to proceed, you are not alone. What this boils down to is that God is there also, but this thought comes in a form that is unprecedented. It is tailor made for your location.

It was a German theologian who first uttered the words, "God is at the center of the world outside the church."[1] He set them in motion in 1945, and, as you will discern, they are something of an enigma to clergy persons. Since you are in the world all week, however, their content is apropos. Clergy and parishioners are accustomed to assuming that God is in church, practically holed up there from Monday through Saturday, only working on Sunday. But that was not what Rev. Dietrich Bonhoeffer had in mind.

That he "relocated God" is a strange way of putting it, because while Hitler was busy invading other countries, and relocating the Jews, the Christian Church did nothing to protest it. From 1939 to 1945, God did not seem to be in the world or of it.

Relocating God is a strange notion because if there is any power that is beyond manipulating or pushing around by humans, it is the Creator. We are talking about One who is on both ends of a light year, of all light years, at the same time. Billions of galaxies and suns orbit in the universe giving astronomers something to gaze at and wonder about. Indeed, the distance light travels in a year is incomprehensible to us, as is the thought that God is One who never eats or sleeps. What is closer to our imagination is to recall that it took the first satellite that reached Mars over six years to get there. The size of the universe is infinite. So the daily workplace is not too far off.

Bonhoeffer was not thinking of light years when he perceived of God being at the center of the weekday world, but it adds to our perception. What he also tells us in his theological writing is that "we live before God as if we were without God."[2] What he meant by this underscores what we already know and are saying when we observe how no one has ever seen God or heard God speak. His statement was a combination of reason, faith, and experience. But once the air is cleared on that score, we at least know what the approach is.

We do not feel God at work within us, for his thoughts can influence ours without our even realizing it, but influence us they do, and once a concept like grace takes up cerebral residence, we begin to see it everywhere. Its properties breed excitement, for they have a way of settling the question what *kind* of a God is at work in the world. The next chapter will attempt to make this clear by contrast. It paves the way for five chapters on grace. Up to now, we have alluded to it, touched upon it, but not really explored it.

"What I like about this book is the way it relates unmerited grace to my daily work experiences. When I leave church my faith has someplace to go that matters. This can happen because grace not only applies to the clergy at a difficult time, but it can enrich a pastor's selection of sermon texts. I agree that if lay people heard more grace on Sunday, they would have a reason to get up not only for church, but on Monday for work.

I underlined all over the manuscript because the language was laden with meaning, e.g. describing wrath and mercy in Chapter 7 as such basic biblical ideas that "lesser ones are traceable to them like limbs on trees." It was a new thought to reflect in Chapter 10 on how Jesus' work in Nazareth prepared him for his public ministry. Also, I am anti-jock but I found the sports section in Chapter 9 compelling. Definitely a keeper.

Unions have humanized performance reviews where I work, but being on a salary I get no overtime pay, so the author's description of work as a "tyranny" fits my life. It also fits single mothers, or both parents working, or fathers working two jobs to make ends meet. Then, too, management that asks for worker input, only to disregard it, drives people up a wall.

In forty years I have never once heard the word "capitalism" mentioned in church. Yet, it is the air I breathe every day. The author admits that losing a sale is more a sin against stockholders than against God, but with gentle irony he adds that wherever support in the midst of failure shows up, the undeserved nature of grace has appeared. I've never read words like that. It's as if the workplace was God's habitat. An awesome idea."

**Cindy Zafft, doctoral candidate employed by the
World Education Corporation**

THE BOSS AND THE FOREMAN

6

IN THE GOSPELS THERE are numerous stories, called parables, wherein characters or ideas from daily life are used to tell the tale. In this chapter, we have used this technique to try and illuminate what happened on the cross between God and Jesus. God is the "Boss" and Jesus the "Foreman." There are two ways this can go, represented here by two scenarios. They are in contrast. The first shows the action moving from the Foreman to the Boss, whereas the second reverses this order and has the action flowing from the Boss through the Foreman, to the workers. In the first the Foreman placates the ire of the Boss, whereas in the second there isn't any ire to placate.

When the parable shifts to *italics* it brings in biblical context.

The key issue is trust. Which Boss can be trusted to remain faithful to the workers through the various changes in society over time?

SCENARIO ONE

In this portrayal, a contract (*covenant*) has been established between the Boss of the corporation and the workers. They agree to work eight hours a day in exchange for wages, safe working conditions, benefits, and other protections. One item in the contract immediately leaps out at readers. The workers must pledge their loyalty to the Boss above all other loyalties. The Foreman, who knows the Boss well, feels constrained to add that the Boss is a jealous man (*Exodus*

34:14). He will not tolerate pictures of family on the desks or pinups on work area walls. He says they are distractions, but to some this seems like the height of superficiality. Many go along with it, a few do not.

The Boss emits an air of authority, which conveys the impression, "I'm in charge." Talking with him is like walking on eggshells. One weighs one's words; the resulting behaviorisms finding their way into our language: "kowtow," "butter up," "stay on the good side," and others that are crude.

As time unfolds the workers get restless. Pay scales based on the estimated value of the employee to the company don't go over well. Workers themselves become jealous, especially when they hear of others getting more money. Some begin to check out the want ads in the paper for other jobs. When the Boss learns of this, a slow burn takes hold within him. For some reason there seems to be an increasing number of workers calling in sick on Fridays and Mondays, and this eats away at the Boss also. When things do not improve, he begins to nurse a grudge, thinking he had done right by the workers in the initial contract relationship. He stays in his office more and the workers hardly ever see him.

Acting as a liaison between the Boss and the workers, the Foreman sets out to try and change the laborers' attitude. He wants to explain how the Boss feels and why. It doesn't go well. A handful of workers listen and agree to cooperate, but certain individuals prod the majority into reacting negatively to the Foreman's efforts. Indeed, they attack him; beat him up with their fists. One gets a tire iron from the trunk of his car and hits him with it. Their own anger gets out of control. The Foreman, on the other hand, has a great deal of patience plus a high pain threshold. He likes the workers, and wanting to win them over, does not retaliate. He does not call for help, when he easily could. He ends up getting killed for his efforts.

While this response to the Foreman is taking place, the Boss watches from his office window several stories above the yard. Gazing down on the labor force, at first he gets even angrier, but then he starts eyeing the Foreman more closely. Something deep within him is touched by what he sees. His wrath toward the workers melts away, and when the Foreman dies, the Boss' anger dies also; he sees the Foreman's death as a supreme sacrifice. The Foreman comes across as a substitute for the people who should really be punished for what they did.

In the 53rd Chapter of Isaiah, a suffering servant is described, one who is beaten by people, but the irony is that the people assume the servant is "stricken and smitten by God," not just by the human beings who imposed the punishment.

The Gospels of Matthew and Mark describe what happened on the cross in terms of a ransom, but interpreters vary on who pays whom. Some say the ransom is paid by God to the Devil, while others say Jesus paid the ransom to God, the payment being his suffering and death. The word "ransom" only appears once, so it is not vested with importance. Other theories carry more weight—sacrifice, satisfaction, and substitution. They have a common theme: Jesus offers himself to God to placate God's wrath.

In theological terms, the action of the Foreman, alias Jesus, satisfies some deep irrational urge the Boss has to punish, but there is no grace in him. Instead, we are left wondering what kind of a father would derive satisfaction from watching his own son being punished for something the son did not do. The Prodigal's father, recall, refused to punish his son for what he *did* do.

Presumably, the sight of his own son being willing to suffer and die for the sins of others moves God deeply, as deeply as he was previously offended. What this suggests is that God had a change of heart, that he was converted. The victory over revenge that Jesus displayed in his crucifixion becomes God's victory also; God is enabled by Jesus' sacrifice to rise above himself. He is redeemed from the feelings he had and, having experienced a change of heart, he can forgive the world.

Here the trust issue enters. For Fundamentalists, the trust is transferred to Jesus. The cross makes Jesus their personal Savior, and for them, the greater the pain of Jesus the greater the salvation.

What is said is that his death saves us from the wages of sin. What is not said, but lurks in the immediate background, is that this Jesus also saves us from the wrath of God. People who do what *this* God does are called schizophrenic or psychotic. One never knows when they will explode. This God would carry such a potential threat in his case file.

To Roman Catholics, when the presiding priest lifts up the bread and wine in the Mass, it changes into the body and blood of Christ. Believing this happens elicits awe from the faithful. Some might interpret this as the priest offering Christ to God, an unbloody symbol of the historic death of Jesus. What is left unasked or unsaid is why the priest offers Christ to God, why it is called the "Sacrifice of the Mass?" The answer to that "why?" lies somewhere in Scenario One.

Translating this to the workplace today, the term "go-between" is relevant. The boss who demands loyalty and who is not easy to please requires a union steward, or some other emissary from the workers, to help arbitrate disputes and negotiate contracts. Even the presence of a union carries the underlying message that things are not exactly copasetic in the workplace between management and labor. *On one occasion in the story of Israel, Moses acts like a union steward and pleads with God to not be angry with the people (Exodus 32:11).*

In these theories—sacrifice, satisfaction, and substitution—God shares the focus with Jesus. However, this focus is founded on three things. One, God, being God, is in such a powerful position. Two, human beings have not delivered the obedience that God demands. And three, the God of justice insists on punishment. Conflict management—taught in seminaries and business schools—was not an option open to Jesus, though it is for management and labor.

SCENARIO TWO

In this explanation of what happened on the cross, the backdrop is at first similar to Scenario One, but with one exception. The Boss and the Foreman have had numerous conversations. There is oneness between them, and the Foreman knows how much the Boss actually loves the workers. Both sense that life is not easy for people, that it brings much pain and suffering. From here on, what happens to the Foreman is the same as in Scenario One and need not be repeated here. What makes this scenario different is the response of the Boss.

As the Boss watches from the window he easily puts himself in the place of both the Foreman and the workers. It is a kind of tragedy for which he assumes the responsibility.

In biblical terms, "If God is for us who can be against us?" Paul once asked his readers. It was a rhetorical question allowing him to declare that "nothing can separate us from God's love," (Romans 8). He then lists a host of things that include beatings, persecution, and suffering of all kinds. However, there is no "smitten by God" here. It is a new approach, a challenge to a long-standing paradigm.

In theological terms, instead of God waiting to be approached by a mediator, God assumes the initiative. He is already on our side, having come to us; intercessory prayers are not necessary.

The image of the corporation head leaving his office and moving out where his people are at work, mingling with employees each day when they had their morning break, for instance, is apropos.

Another New Testament writer who takes up this new theme is John. He sounds as if he is aware of some murky depth in God that needs to be overcome or changed. He observes how God is light and in him is no darkness at all (1:5). It is an expression of language dedicated to the proposition that God is singularly one with Jesus and with us.

In other words, there is no schizophrenia in God. He is not psychotic. What we have in the Second Scenario is a God who cares. God is not receiving anything. Nothing is being offered to God. Then, just to make sure no one fails to understand this point, or writes it off as a fine line, *Paul pens these words to the Corinthians, "All this is from God, who through Christ reconciled us to himself . . . that is, God was in Christ reconciling the world to himself" (II Corinthians 5:18-*

19). God was in Jesus from the start. He was doing it not to reconcile himself to the world—getting over some kind of grudge as it were—but reconciling the world to himself. The action begins and ends with God. There is nothing anyone can add to it or take away. It is an accomplished fact. It never needs to be repeated. It is visible redemption but with the Invisible God in full participation. God does not need a change of heart.

What God does through Jesus demonstrates how far forgiveness will go. The one who is present in and with Jesus on the cross is the God of grace. God is the initiator, participant, and revealer simultaneously.

Thus, not only was Jesus suffering on the cross, but the Unseen God was there, suffering, also. What we have here is the capacity of the Almighty to sense pain, to experience forsakenness, alienation, and rejection. It is by God's stripes that we are healed; he is the suffering servant. Since God is light, there is no darkness in him.

In terms of the Boss and Foreman parable, we might imagine a situation in which someone brings charges against the man who killed the Foreman with the tire iron. It is an open and shut case; too many people saw it happen. The jury agrees. However, when it comes time for the judge to pass sentence, there is a stirring in the courtroom. The Boss rises from his seat and walks down the aisle to where the convicted killer is waiting to hear what will happen to him. The Boss looks at the man and says, "You are free to go." Then the Boss takes his place and accepts the verdict upon himself. It is the moment when he accepts the responsibility. It is an example of vicarious suffering. It is unconditional, unmerited grace at work.[1]

This God does not have to have human beings pounding away on his son in order to be inwardly moved. It isn't only to Jesus that his heart goes out. It is to all of humanity who suffer and die one by one or in groups, on this planet. We often think we are alone, that somehow we have done something to deserve our plight, but the boardroom to which God extends his arms is worldwide.

It is God's will that Jesus suffer and die, but not to satisfy any desire for justice. It is not a demonstration of God's wrath over human sin, but an attempt to reveal the extent to which God will go to redeem the world, to reconcile the world to himself. "There's a kindness in God's justice that is more than liberty," as the hymn writer expresses it.

Top officials in a corporation accept the fact that the organizational chart places them in a position of responsibility. However, taking a cue from God's compassion, this is not an opportunity for exploiting managerial privileges but rather, for appreciating the time and effort of the entire workforce in bringing profit to the company. By this, a sense of oneness can develop in the company.

CONVERSATION STARTERS

FOR CHAPTER 6

⟨?⟩ In what way is the difference between the two bosses and the two deities an issue of the heart?

⟨?⟩ In what ways are the two bosses and the two deities blessed or cursed with their frame of mind?

⟨?⟩ How do you feel about the Bible itself describing these two views as the difference between darkness and light?

⟨?⟩ How would the CEO and his management peers lift the morale of the workforce by reaching out to them and treating them as human beings, like themselves?

⟨?⟩ In what way is the difference we are describing here one of putting people first and law second?

⟨?⟩ Would it take weakness or strength to do what Boss did in the courtroom scene?

⟨?⟩ Is it necessary to have trust in the workplace? How might this chapter inspire that trust, starting with the book or the pulpit?

Under New Management

7

In Chapter 5's "Memo to the CEO," we introduced Bonhoeffer's idea that God was at the center of the weekday world, including the workplace, but we said little about what that God was like there. It was a general observation like the umbrella "In God we trust," stamped on U.S. coins, or the words "under God" in our Pledge to the Flag. They do not divulge what kind of a God we are talking about, either. In Chapter 6, two basic attributes were considered, wrath and mercy, and in this chapter, we shall apply these terms to the workplace.

For example, fifty workers watched and listened to the motors that generate electricity throughout the flight for commercial airplanes. They were making sure the flaps, lights, air conditioning, heating units, and landing gear would have power along with sending it to the jet engine starter motors. If there were any problems they showed up on computerized data tapes. The men were testers for the Sundstrand Corporation.

The testers could easily read the tapes, but Sundstrand employed six inspectors to perform this task, and their word was law. If they were in a bad mood from a quarrel a home, they often transferred it to the tapes and found things wrong that were not there. This possibility filled the room with stress and resentment as if wrath were an employee at Sundstrand waiting to strike an angry note.

A change occurred when another corporation, Hamilton, became joint owners. The strained relationships in the generator shop were seen as counterproductive. Under new management, different work was found for the inspectors, and the task of reading the data was given to the testers. Hamilton understood the human situation, but it was like divine mercy entering that division of the corporation. The egos, thoughts, and abilities of the testers were recognized and appreciated.

The wrath we are alluding to here is not the hell-fire kind that emanates from many TV evangelists, but the belief that the Creator has designed humanity with certain people lording it over others so that fear and intimidation gets things done. The "lords" have more responsibility, make the decisions, and are paid more. Inequality was set in motion by God, and even the church bears witness to it in its hierarchical organizational structure. This is the old management and it is rather prevalent still.

The new management, illustrated by the Hamilton Corporation, sees how wrath undermines relationships, whereas understanding (a component of mercy) reinforces them. In other words, it helps if the workplace functions as a family, a primary group, a place where trust prevails, and its members do not have to always guard what they say. Starbucks is such a corporation, as is Southwest Airlines. In a TV program featuring the most efficient businesses in the U.S., the narrator asked a Starbucks' employee if he loved his boss. At first the young man hesitated, not sure perhaps how the answer would be taken. Finally he replied in the affirmative, and it seemed like something from a family. But, what a climate in which to work!

EXPANSION

One of the insights the Bush Administration has bequeathed to the U.S. is that unilateral decision-making is not the path to pursue. It invites blame if things do not go well; critics hunt for someone to hold accountable. The converse of this is that it pays to have allies when one embarks on a new course of action. Indeed, one of the first places mercy demonstrates itself is in decision-making.

When it comes to organizations, the way decisions are arrived at is as important as the decision itself. The by-products contribute to the on-going effectiveness or ineffectiveness of the business.

For example, ecclesiastical corporations are known to function with what are called "executive sessions," the name being a derivative from the participants—CEO and other management persons. The doors to the room are closed, and when I once worked in such a place, they even taped brown paper over the windows, apparently so we could not walk by and read lips. What the scene made one aware of was being an outsider. Feeling ostracized, the mind assumes that secrets are being discussed. Trust on the part of employees is undermined. However ironic it may be, like a conclave in the Vatican to elect a pope, once that decision was reached it could be shared.

Intensifying the negative reaction to the executive session model of decisionmaking in the above religious corporation was an effort at restructuring involving the assignment of a value to each person's work. This value indicated how much he or she was worth to the church, i.e., how much each would be paid.

In secular corporate boardrooms, issues are also discussed behind closed doors, and once a decision has been made it can be revealed. The process is a secret not the result. An example of a decision arrived at this way occurred some years ago in Detroit's General Motor Corporation. The issue being discussed was whether to shut down the Flint, Michigan plant. The decision to close it was devastating to the city, putting many people out of work.

The irony is that corporation officials are paid big sums of money to make these decisions, and often they have resulted in laying-off large numbers of people, closing stores, and shutting down factories, to reduce overhead and stave off bankruptcy. We read about this with dismay, for many families are suddenly minus money to make ends meet. The salaries of those making the decisions, however, are usually protected.

We do not know whether the decisions are arrived at dispassionately, but there is no doubt about their effect on the minds of employees.

When close friends lose their jobs, or paychecks do not include the raises others receive, one feels like anger has motivated the decision. "What did I do to deserve this?" is a response that often follows something considered unfair.

In corporate boardrooms across the globe there could be an alternative to the decisions regarding a downside in profit and income. The CEO and other well-paid officials could take pay cuts so that workers would not have to be laid off. Some would call this loyalty and quip that loyalty up requires loyalty down.

In 2004, Delta Airlines asked its pilots to take a thirty-five percent cut in their $300,000 dollar salaries, but the pilots would only go up to nine percent. Actually, Delta was lucky to get that. Management did not lead the way by announcing its own pay cuts. In fact, top management people were offered bonuses to stay but four of them left anyway for greener runways.

Curiously, the tendency of Moses to make unilateral decisions, or to involve no one but his brother, Aaron, and occasionally their sister Miriam, prompted the same kind of reaction in 600 BCE that we can find today in U.S. corporations. At that time it led to Korah's rebellion. Korah was a member of the Tribe of Levi, and as such was already on the inside when it came to what God wanted. What Korah did not like was the way Moses excluded everyone outside his own family when it came to the decision-making process.

The protest began with Korah camping on the doorstep of Moses with 250 other well-known leaders in the Hebrew community. It was perhaps the first union protest against management, a biblical archetype.

The initial response of Moses was to be "very angry" (Numbers 16:15), but God not only surprisingly concurred, he also declared his intention to consume the Levitical "unionizers" on the spot. However, the writer of the account reports Moses interceding for the people. He asked God, "wilt one man sin and you are angry with them all?" It was one of the little huddles Moses is reported to have with God in the Tent of Meeting, a boardroom made out of cloth, and with no secretary present to hear God's voice or jot down what was said.

The intervention of Moses doesn't do any good. The earth swallows up the Hebrew union members in one gulp, triggering, the very next day, a larger uprising complaining that the punishment was too severe; it did not fit the crime. As a reward for registering their grievance, they, too, were exterminated by God, leaving us to scratch our interpretational heads. One moment Moses is angry. The next, he attempts to reconcile God to the situation, but divine wrath explodes both times. Trusting in divine mercy would be a hard thing to do.

In his Pulitzer Prize winning book, *God: A Biography*, Jack Miles, a former priest, notes in the beginning how despite God's rainbow promise to not destroy the world again, God "remains a permanently threatening presence."[1] And just over half way through the book, he adds in parentheses: "…as we have seen, the Lord is endlessly angry and displeased."[2] The God that Miles writes about is a parent whose children can never please him.

In contrast to the above, broadening the base of support and building trust, would *not* be a difficult process to initiate as far as today's corporate employees are concerned. Many people could be involved in decision-making, one way being the referendum approach states use every four years, placing before voters something to which reaction is sought.

CEO's who assume this would be like making policy in the street would benefit from asking a small group to consider a problem related to their field of work and then assessing the quality of the feedback.

Once the top management people are convinced that workers have minds as well as bodies, they could organize the company into small teams for issue-oriented conversation. Keeping the group size under ten would assure greater participation, and make it possible for self-confidence and a sense of worth to play a motivating part. No doubt there would be some dissenters, but with everybody invited to the party, there will be more supporters and fewer foot draggers. Company morale will increase whereas with unilateral decisions it decreases. The bottom line here is that high morale leads to motivation.

Other kinds of problems could be alleviated from broadening the base of decision-making. It might even help avoid suits for accidents and negligence. Unilateral decision-making destroys the climate in a group of people that see each other every day, whereas involving them, taking mercy into account, restores and enhances relationships.

MOTIVATION

Wrath and mercy provide two biblical directions. They are such basic attributes that lesser ones are traceable to them, like limbs on trees. They are opposites that do not attract. Indeed, they repel each other and give the Creator the impression of suffering from schizophrenia, with which we will have to deal.

The motivations implicit in wrath and mercy surface in their meanings, and providing help in that regard is the dictionary. Actually, in any dictionary "wrath" means intense anger, rage, or fury, dispensed for purposes of punishment. When "anger" is used instead of "wrath" in the Bible, it is often preceded by the word "fierce," to keep the fire hot.

"Mercy," on the other hand, is defined as refraining from punishing enemies, kindness in excess of what may be expected and a disposition to forgive, all three of which are the antithesis of wrath, the epitome of grace. Indeed, mercy is the Hebrew prelude to the grace found in the Christian portion of the Bible.

Both of these two approaches could relate to common corporation problems, such as gender harassment, or that of a boss. Responding to these injustices out of anger might provide a momentary satisfaction of paying back, but to anticipate a well-known verse, "A soft answer turns away wrath," mercy is the way to go, and this occurs when one sits down and talks the issue over with the one who is perpetrating it. This is mercy because the harasser perhaps deserves some kind of reprisal, but forgoing this natural inclination for a quiet conversation speaks of kindness in the face of what is certainly disturbing.

Professional theologians are inclined to forego the definitions of wrath and mercy, and to advocate instead the use of the word "tension" to describe the relationship between the two. However, tension robs mercy and grace of their power, moving them closer to anger and wrath.

Moreover, tension describes the adversarial relationship within many corporations between union and management. It is not exactly a reconciling dynamic. We will have to move beyond tension to provide Monday morning incentive.

Wrath and mercy are important attributes to distinguish between if for no other reason than that wrath is hard to trust. Lack of trust was what the above generator testers felt with the inspectors looking over their shoulders. The new managerial approach brought to the company by Hamilton showed that they realized the testers were acutely motivated by the reality of airplane passengers depending on them for a safe trip. Moreover, there was a reputation to uphold. As pilots are known to announce when the plane has arrived, "You have just completed the safest part of your journey. We wish you well on the ground."

Actually, there is far more at work in the wrath/mercy contrast than tension. This is evidenced in the Bible itself, where a conflict between the two attributes erupts within its own pages. Deuteronomy 13 records one example in which Moses plays a major role. An incident occurred when the Israelites were entering Canaan with the aim of making it the land God promised them. When idolatry was found in one of the cities of Canaan, it prompts Moses to order the razing of the entire city as a whole burnt offering to God. The report conveys the impression that he speaks for God, but it is not clear whether it is God or Moses who issues the order.

What adds to the issue is that Moses decrees the destruction of a city to appease the fierceness of the Lord's anger *so the Lord can turn from it to mercy*. It presumably takes this scourge of punishment to satisfy divine wrath. God's anger does subside, but the account is tinged with absurdity. After torching the city and annihilating its inhabitants, there is no one left to receive the mercy.

The appearance of the mercy idea hints that deep down Moses knows something is not right with this policy. He may not realize whether it is his own will or God's that gives the order, but wrath prevails either way.

When we read the contents of Scripture carefully, the opposite natures of wrath and mercy show up with regularity. One opposite is that of duration. Wrath or anger are temporary, whereas mercy is eternal. In ten different places mercy is described as "enduring forever." The contrast suggests that the eternal endurance of mercy was a needed alternative to even short term anger. The time contrast also emerges in these words, "For his anger is but for a moment, and his favor is for a lifetime" (Psalm 30:5). Another translation says "God's wrath lasts but for the twinkling of an eye."

The duration of mercy also assumes eternal proportions in Psalm 103:17 where it is "from everlasting to everlasting." It characterizes the beginning and the end, the Alpha and the Omega. For anger to show up in between is an incongruity.

Even within anger itself there is a lack of consistency. In one place anger builds up gradually. In another it erupts suddenly. In the Second Psalm, wrath is kindled quickly but in Nehemiah 9:17 the Lord is described as "slow to anger." Nehemiah joins it to redemptive patience when he writes, "They were a stiff-necked people, but thou art a God ready to forgive, gracious and merciful, *slow to anger,* and abounding in steadfast love." This is unmerited grace emerging in the Hebrew scripture. It bursts forth like a happy surprise.

Against the background of a divine "tantrum," such as led to the destruction of Sodom, the words of Micah are like the calm in a hurricane's eye. "What does the Lord require of you," he asked, "but to do justly, love mercy, and walk humbly with your God." A God that *loves* mercy is quite different from one that vents wrath.

It seems fair to suggest that at the juncture of punishment and pardon, the Bible sends out contradictory signals; if one is true, the other is false. They are mutually exclusive. They are incongruities, not paradoxes. They cannot be written off as *divine* inconsistencies. And to be left with a schizophrenic God is not helpful.

INTERPRETATION

Having questioned the validity of schizophrenia and tension as viable explanations for the contrast of wrath and mercy in the Bible, a more promising interpretation is needed. One possibility is to see them as a mingling of anger and mercy impulses in the minds of biblical writers. The presence of wrath—the intent to punish, and the fierce anger that humans call upon God to explode on their enemies or "wicked" neighbors—could be a projection by these writers. It would then be a mortal grudge extended to an eternal conclusion, like telling someone to "go to hell." It is the all too human way of rationalizing a fit of temper by calling it righteous indignation. God's mercy could be seen as the true nature of God because of its redeeming effects, whereas a God of wrath is a product of human nature raised to the highest power.

Another interpretation is to see divine mercy in the Hebrew Scripture as a breakthrough in the midst of wrath, and with this, the Christian Testament witness to unearned or unmerited grace ties in well. They even share a mathematical dimension. If just a few individuals manifest human sinfulness then we could say there is something wrong with them. Their presence would be no more than coincidental. However, if the presence of sin is universal, then we cannot say it is coincidence. Then we have to consider the cause in weighing the veracity of the claim. That cause is apparent in Paul's observation that "God consigns *all* things to sin." The grace part comes in the next half of the observation, "That [God] might have mercy upon *all*" (Romans 11). Both sides of that statement render grace indispensable, but the keys are in the word *all*.

Closing this chapter with a touch of reality, we would note how, despite an appreciation for unearned grace, both boss and workers can experience anger. Not even the boss who has bought into workplace democracy, servant leadership, or grace in the workplace is going to avoid anger 100 percent of the time. A boss who is angry may want to simmer down before initiating a conversation with the workers who may have triggered it. We don't turn mercy on and off like water from a faucet, but the trickle starts when we realize the need to cool off. While cooling off, some leftover anger may slip out. The good news is that at whatever point we are as human beings, God's grace covers us before, during, and after we have acted.

CONVERSATION STARTERS

FOR CHAPTER 7

What other reasons for secretive executive sessions or boardroom decisions can you think of?

Which of the two deity attributes in the Bible would provide a better policy model for corporations, and why?

How might employer belief in either divine wrath or mercy influence performance reviews?

If mercy is from everlasting to everlasting, how could the idea of divine wrath ever get there in between?

If "all" does not mean *all,* what does it mean?

"In fifty plus years of ministry in the Church, I had never given thought to the idea that 'grace' has a necessary workplace dimension as well as a personal one. However, I was raised on the idea of being pious on Sunday but working hard during the week. Johnson helps active pastors and seminarians preparing for parish ministry to apply Bonhoeffer's idea that God is in the center of the weekday world. It is good to know that we are valued by the 'power' whom we name God. When we think about it, It makes no sense to assume that 'grace' is just a Sunday word.

The Word does join pulpit and pew, but I like the author's observation that when those in the pews who are members of the workforce hear thoughts on a subject that genuinely interests them, they listen more and can take the message home. I wish I had read this book fifty years ago. Good thing that I am saved by grace, too."

Gordon S. Nelson, Retired Pastor
West Barnstable, Massachusetts

THE NAME OF THE rock group I forget, but I recall from a music review that they were loud. When the last of their decibel breaking sound died out, and they had vacated the stage, a black woman approached the microphone. It was Jessie Norman, the opera singer. She began softly, singing "Amazing Grace." At first there were some boos. "We want rock" was heard. When she got to the second stanza the noise quieted down, and when she commenced the third, one could hear the proverbial pin drop.

The setting was not a church but an outdoor half shell, and the audience was not assembled for a religious purpose. Yet they responded positively, even to the thought that grace "saved a wretch like me." It's easier accepting the word "wretch" out in the world than in church, and hearing "Amazing Grace" sung in baseball stadiums, at a Ground Zero ceremony, as well as at a rock concert, has the overtone of a national hymn.

THE POLICE DEPARTMENT

The reader may recall how taking unmerited grace seriously was difficult for lawyers and law enforcement people in the 16th Century time of Martin Luther (Chapter 4). To do so, they had to keep it in church and apart from their daily work. It is still hard for prosecuting attorneys and the police to relate to free grace today, unless they live in Japan.

In the States, the police major in threat and intimidation, unless they are called to a car accident involving injuries. In Japan, the policy with citizens guilty of misdemeanors is one of building rapport.

The primary purpose of Japan's criminal justice system is not to punish, but to cultivate respect for the law. They do this by showing what amounts to sympathy for people enmeshed in a crime. Only by letting the "warm blood flow," as they put it, will offenders learn to respect the law and its agents. Police officers are recognized for the nature of their care not the severity of their response. It may seem they are soft on crime, but as we shall note, the results speak for themselves.

The way in which this dynamic unfolds is in the extending of conditional forgiveness to the lawbreaker, the most important criterion for receiving this being an act of contrition by the offender. As one observer has written, "The Japanese law-enforcement system does not apply punishment to fit the crime, but rather, to fit the demeanor of the culprit after the crime."[1] This is a bit different from the United States, where, at the behest of lawyers, lawbreakers can be caught red-handed and still plead "not guilty."

Contrition that is deemed sincere can end the matter. For example, the owner of a bicycle stolen by a teenager refused to prosecute a "child." Because the boy seemed truly sorry, the police, too, refused to press the matter. Charges were also dropped against a university student caught shoplifting 9,000 Yen-worth of phonograph records. Why? He had no previous criminal record, and was very repentant.

Apology is one form of repentance. Written apologies are widely used by the police in dealing with certain kinds of crime, as in the case where a man was coercing a woman into having sex. The woman was both furious and scared. The officers arranged that if he apologized to the woman and wrote a letter saying he would not do it again, the woman would not press charges. However, Japanese police are well aware that contrition can be feigned and their goodwill abused. Thus, one value of written apologies is that those of repeat offenders accumulate in a folder, providing the police with grounds for prosecution. In murder cases, however, prosecution is mandatory. Felonies are not simply "forgiven."

In Japan there is unusual cooperation between police and prosecutors, in that four-fifths of the suspects in serious crimes are prosecuted without arrest. Most suspects accept responsibility for their actions and cooperate voluntarily in their own prosecution in the way described above. By comparison, in the States, arrest is the beginning of a criminal case.

One reason this works in Japan is that for a Japanese person, saving face is practically a cultural norm. To be caught is embarrassing enough. Further punishment would only add insult to injury. Thus, in Japan imprisonment is used much more sparingly than in the United States. Moreover, prison sentences are shorter. The incarceration rate in the States is five times greater than it is in Japan, and the murder rate eleven times more, on a per capita basis.

It is difficult to pinpoint how the Japanese came by this redemptive approach to crime. However, they did not get it from Christianity. As a religion, Christianity is embraced by less than one percent of the Japanese population. Whatever its source, this emphasis on redemption has influenced their humanity. We cite it here as an outcropping of unmerited grace in a non-Christian country.

CORPORATIONS

Although "business is business" still gives daily work a hard nose, and unions and management still have adversarial relationships, a new dimension has entered the workplace, thanks to W. Edwards Deming mentioned in Chapter 5. It's no wonder his non-adversarial approach to daily work became known as "workplace democracy." While he was alive, it caught on in seven hundred American companies. A major theme in his "gospel" was that corporate policies designed to scare workers are counterproductive. These policies include rules, regulations, inspections, and annual performance reviews that put laws above people. Deming reversed this and placed people above laws, much as Jesus did when he said the Sabbath was made for man, not man for the Sabbath.

Mention was made in Chapter 2 of the Dana Corporation, where sixty-three thousand employees have been exposed to the Deming approach in corporation management. Its "mission statement" declares that "we are dedicated to the belief that our people are our most important asset."[2] In a few paragraphs this declaration replaced a stack of corporate procedures that looked like the Book of Leviticus.

When Jesus said that "lording it over others" was not a good idea, he was favoring a redistribution of power, something many CEO's in church and society find hard to do. Democracy in the workplace involves the transition from boss to colleague. What happens when the leader serves as a resource rather than an order-giver is that the organizational chart is visually reversed. "Our hierarchy is just like that of any other plant," said Dennis Butt of Kawasaki, "except that I turned it upside down. My position is on the bottom of the chart and the hourly worker's is on the top. Everyone else is here to support him or her."[3]

Where grace shows up in the workplace, the leader views the redistribution of power not as a surrender, but as a sharing. It is a sign of strength not weakness, says Peter Gyllenhammar, president of Volvo. "The weak are incapable of delegating and have every reason to fear sharing their power. The strong have the self-confidence that makes delegation possible and easy."[4]

Replacing fear with grace in the workplace means allowing room for failure. In describing how the Jones and Laughlin Steel Corporation increased production at a Cleveland mill by 20 percent, the president said success came from "deep delegation" of authority to superintendents, which left management "free to make [the] big mistakes."[5] Since decision making is also at the mill floor level, workers, too, are in the position of asserting initiative, stumbling, recovering, and trying again.

Failure in the workplace, however, often means falling short of company standards. "Sin" may be losing a sale or not meeting a deadline. As such, it is more of a sin against the stockholders or the profit motive than against God. Nonetheless, however secular such sins may seem, wherever they are forgiven, grace is there also. This grace may occur in a steel mill, but it is still grace at work. Daily life, not one hour in church on Sunday, is the arena in which the Word of God's unmerited mercy applies. Wherever support in the midst of failure shows up, it is unmerited, undeserved. The nature of grace redeems the nature of failure.

What this says is that come Monday morning motives other than greed are alive in the human spirit. Grace is not given just to an elite group of believers who meet in church; everybody who gets up in the morning is under the influence, and grace does not come to an end after breakfast. Neither is there need to think that if threat and exhortation are removed, workers will cease being motivated. As Rene McPherson, former Dean of Stanford Business School, observed, "We don't motivate people. They are motivated by their upbringing, education, and other things. What we are doing is taking the handcuffs off . . . ." [6]

The foundation for grace appearing in daily life is that in God we live, move, and have our being all week long, whether acknowledged or not. Where grace is, God is. There is no grace apart from God and no God apart from grace. What God gives on Sunday through Word and Sacrament—or wants to give—is faith and reason, awareness of what God gives all week.

One example of how corporate grace is at work without being recognized, relates to the pay chasm between labor and management. Day after day the hourly workers show up and do their job knowing all the time that the CEO and other management persons make huge sums of money, thanks to the accumulative effects of all their hourly work. Perhaps fear keeps the latter group from rebelling, but the effect is that of undeserved grace shown to those whose incomes are inflated.

This example of corporate grace could be nicely supplemented by those making millions in management positions sharing more of the profits with those hourly workers who make them rich. It becomes grace because those higher up the ladder are inclined to believe that those beneath them do not *deserve* such increments in pay. Since grace, by definition, is undeserved, to make the income levels more even would be tantamount to a kind of gift from the top to the bottom.

The infusion of undeserved grace into the corporate layers would do a lot for the morale of the organization because of the way it ties in with a bedrock ingredient of the human personality, namely, self-esteem. An apt translation of this term for our purposes is *self-worth*. The notion that we only gain this by self-achievement is a misunderstanding of the grace of God. It implies that the Creator does not know how important self-esteem is to our well-being. To say that the grace of God undermines self-worth is also unfair to both grace and God.

Although human achievement is satisfying, in relation to God, there is an added dimension, call it a redemptive side effect. It comes when we know we are valued by the "highest power." Grace provides this. We see that the Author of Life does understand our needs and has not hidden within grace some kind of negative side effect. Grace bestows a sense of worth precisely because it is undeserved.

The value of self-esteem and self-worth has been well documented in the lives of children, but in focusing on *them* we may have overlooked the extent to which we are still children when we reach much older ages.

When self-esteem is not nurtured it leaves a void inside, and it easily leads to hostility that an adult can transfer to the corporation. Conversely, an increase in pay that comes from profit sharing at the top comes across as appreciation because it is a tangible way of saying "thanks." Workers at the bottom of the pay scale get a sense of belonging to the company. Loyalty has a chance to develop, and taking more pride in one's work, the quality improves, all because a measure of self-worth has been tapped by grace. Calling in sick might decrease.

Workers that are the quickest to protest unfair labor practices might lose the ardor for such responses when their own self-worth has been increased. The child within is waiting to gain recognition. The scars of youth are in the memory system, and behavior functions as a pain signal. But the grace of God suggests that healing is never too late.

Lack of self-esteem means that a person has become alienated from him or herself. When this happens, the only source of self-worth left may be the grace of God. Society may be insensitive to a person's background, but God is well informed.

Management that incorporates this into its policy making is doing itself a favor. Those at the top who make the huge incomes would receive a greater sense of self-respect and thus self-esteem knowing that they are contributing to the overall morale of the corporation. Everybody wins!

THE SPORTS WORLD

Grace operates in the athletic department both in spontaneous circumstances and in organized forms. It can occur privately in a locker room or in broad daylight in full view of thousands of people. In 1990, Bill Buckner awaited baseball's opening day at Fenway Park in Boston with a sinking feeling in the pit of his stomach. Just a few years before, a ball want through his legs at first base when he bent forward to catch it, costing the Red Sox the World Series. He was subsequently traded in disgrace. In 1990, as a free agent, he had asked for the chance to try out for the team in Spring training. Perhaps he wanted to redeem himself. He did make the team, and when, on opening day, his name was announced over the public address system he received a standing ovation. Part of this could be that the press had applauded his courage to even show his face back in Boston. However, something else was at work here—grace, forgiveness even. He was in need of reconciliation and he received it. He did not redeem himself.

Often it can be a series of team mistakes that contribute to a loss. On the other hand, there are times when one individual's mistake results in the whole team losing. The one who is the goat may hear about it when the team meets, but frequently we observe on the playing field how a teammate goes out of his way to provide solace for the person who just blew the play. Sometimes a coach will take the blame for a loss, whether it was his fault or not. When that occurs, so has the grace of God.

We are not saying that unmerited grace is recognized as such. However, recognized or not, grace has an effect on the team; it is a source of oneness. As such, it is the glue that holds athletes together, especially in a sport where a few receive most of the credit and many plod through a season with little or no fan recognition. In football, runners, quarterbacks, and wide receivers receive acclaim, but neither runners nor quarterbacks would do much if it were not for the linemen who open holes or protect the passer.

What makes this grace, on the part of the linemen, is that deserving more credit than they receive, they continue to contribute to the team's effort. To be unrecognized or unacknowledged and yet to give oneself to a cause is grace, whether it be true of God or human beings.

To someone who feels that money is what renews a professional athlete's spirit, it could be pointed out that the higher the salary the greater the pressure to perform, to demonstrate one deserves it, and the greater the guilt in failure. Following this line of thought, slumps, mistakes, and errors by high-priced stars only intensify the need for renewal of the spirit from some other source than money. In this chapter, that other source is the grace of forgiveness. Should animosity or envy replace it, the team's glue simply dries up.

*   *   *

As noted above, grace under the pressure of sports can also be organized. In team cycling, we see this at work. One member of the team is selected ahead of time to "win" while the others are "horses." Some team members are responsible for taking an early lead to tire out the opposition. Others stay back and provide a slip stream or draft for the designated winner, so he can conserve energy. Still, others take their turn in front to cut through the wind. Then, at the last one hundred yards, the team opens a hole for the winner. Full of energy, he or she breaks away to the finish line and receives the award alone. In many ways the award is undeserved. The winner did not work for it the way the others did. It is a kind of gift—grace. While it is an organized, team effort, it is a tale on a deeper level than sports.

In bowling and golf it is both common and acceptable to ask, "What is your handicap?" The use of a handicap is to compensate a player for his or her lesser ability in relation to others. What it boils down to is a gift, designed to make competition more even and therefore more interesting. It is not a question of receiving something because of an achievement. The whole idea of achievement is stood on its head. One could say a person is recognized for underachievement given a handicap because of a sub-par performance. Only in a mathematical sense is the handicap merited. The advantage it gives is unmerited. Nonetheless, however it is labeled, it is an example of organized grace.

To a person accustomed to keeping grace in a religious building mediated by ordained clergy, referring to grace in the world may seem like heresy, as if it should not be there. However, a coach or a teammate who says, "Don't worry about it, we'll do better next time," is tapping the same reservoir of reconciliation as the clergy person who says to a parishioner, "Your sins are forgiven." To be sure, an error at first base is hardly a sin against God, but for Boston fans it was unforgivable, until Someone entered with a magnanimous spirit. Alienation and estrangement among human beings needs the breakthrough that comes from grace just as much as does separation from God. And if we do live and have our being in God, then God, too, suffers when human beings are separated. Moreover, God is affirmed in this book as the source of all reconciliation, wherever it happens to appear.

CONVERSATION STARTERS

FOR CHAPTER 8

Is it easier to accept the word "wretch" in a secular setting than in church? If so, why?

What part do lawyers play in preventing the "warm blood" between police and citizens to flow here in the States?

Which policy in "workplace democracy" comes closest to the teachings of Jesus alluded to in this chapter?

Does God need or depend on Sacraments in order to go to work in human beings during the week?

How might team spirit be on a deeper level than sports?

Why would the grace of God contribute to self-esteem or self-worth?

9

"WILL GOD FORGIVE A person for making the increase of profit a lifelong pursuit"? Seventy-eight percent of the respondents in the Sunday/Monday study referred to in Chapter 2 were not sure. They had never heard anyone from the "church" raise the issue or respond to it. They were people directly involved in setting the prices, such as doctors, lawyers, business and sales persons, and those in the technical professions. They were not CEOs who supplemented their million-dollar incomes with the investment money of stockholders. They were just ordinary people with average incomes, all beneficiaries of grace in the workplace.

When what one does eight hours a day raises the question whether God forgives us for the profit we make from it, the situation is serious. It is impossible to survive in the modern world without capitalism, and the profit margin is, indeed, a dilemma. Whether the price being charged is too high or too low, it can either undercut business or drive one out of it. Grace in the pulpit would cultivate discussion about daily work, but we have to rethink "cheap grace" first.

RETHINKING CHEAP GRACE

In addition to a paucity of grace themes in sermon text selection, another reason grace seldom gets even honorable mention is that it is regarded as "cheap." The label appeared around 1937, when German theologian, Dietrich Bonhoeffer, published his book *The Cost of Discipleship.* Just for the record, the context for his phrase "cheap grace" is that of public worship, where corporate confession is part of the liturgical agenda. Either declaring "forgiveness without requiring repentance" or offering "absolution without contrition" is his definition of "cheap grace."[1]

We need to rethink his declaration, if for no other reason than the chain reaction it has first on the pulpit and then on society itself. In April of 2004, Peter Jennings narrated a three-hour program entitled *Jesus and Paul,* which was quite well done. Two of the hours were on Paul, but not one reference to Paul's emphasis on the grace of God was made. The focus on Paul was on his ethical rules of conduct for the congregations he started and then wrote to. Either the theological and biblical advisers to the program kept quiet about it, or Jennings overruled them, assuming it was unimportant, since he never heard about in sermons.

In rethinking "cheap grace," two questions place it on the pages of this chapter. The first is *How do we measure repentance or contrition?* What are the criteria— words, tears, deeds? How many tears would be enough? What kind of words? And would a worshipper present the pastor with a list of deeds (penance in advance) to demonstrate authenticity?

The second question relates to references in the Gospels to Jesus' parable of the Prodigal Son, and his urging Peter to forgive seventy times seven. There is no hint of contrition being on the father's mind, and when forgiveness adds up to the symbolical figure of 490, not only does the repetition of sins surface, but the difficulty of maintaining contrition throughout becomes formidable. *Was Jesus indulging in "cheap grace" in these two instances?* If so, then we are, at least, in good company, but in this chapter we intend to show that while grace is not cheap for God, it is for us, and understanding that would help relate grace to the workplace scene.

Bonhoeffer's awareness of what he calls "cheap grace" was perhaps influenced by two contrasting experiences, the formality of European corporate worship and the close, personal contact he had with a small group of seminarians he was teaching. In his little gem of a book, *Life Together*, the contrasting experiences come to life.

> Despite corporate worship, the final breakthrough to fellowship does not occur, because, though we have fellowship with one another as believers and as devout people, we do not have fellowship as the undevout, as sinners. The pious fellowship permits no one to be a sinner. So everybody must conceal his sin from himself and from the fellowship.[2]

Then he added, "Many Christians are unthinkably horrified when a real sinner is suddenly discovered among the righteous. So we remain alone with our sin, living in lies and hypocrisy."

Worship becomes a burial ground where anything really troubling us is interred alive, daily work included. When worship is over, a pious façade descends on the community, making grace a stranger to our conversations, removing along with it any concern over God's relation to the necessary pursuit of profit.

Although his reference to "cheap grace" in *The Cost of Discipleship* is a momentary one, Bonhoeffer does disclose his theology behind it. For him, grace is costly *because* it cost God the life of His Son, and what has cost God so much cannot be cheap for us.[3] What it actually cost God we do not know, but whatever it was, it would seem to overlook the difference between God's experience of cost and ours. Moreover, only God knows what it is like to "endure all things" (First Corinthians 13).

We can *say* that it would include an infinite capacity for pain, but finite creatures cannot know what that is. We even erect psychological defenses against suffering to protect ourselves from the fallout. It would seem reasonable to assume that God does not do that. In any event, compared with whatever grace costs God, it *is* inexpensive for us.

THE PAST IS PROLOGUE ONCE MORE

Oddly enough, it is a sin to be a sinner in church, and this absence of a sense of sin in "church" has been noted for some time. As early as the 4th Century there was an awareness of it. The Council of Carthage issued a clear declaration that even *saints* must acknowledge how they are sinners and must always pray, in truth and not merely out of humility, "forgive us our trespasses."[4] The implication here is that while sins are real even for "saints," they were not coming through as real although they, too, were exposed to the real world in working for a living.

Then, one hundred years ago it showed up again when Danish theologian, Soren Kirkegaard, wrote:

> Surely it is an indictment of what passes for Christianity in our age that authentic consciousness of sin is rare. For most people the daily condition of being in sin is so seldom noticed that it has come to be regarded as normal. Only strikingly bad deeds are counted as new sins, and the rest of the time they assume that everything is going moderately well.[5]

As for our economic system, that remains outside the stained-glass window with other topics that hint at moral weakness. Describe capitalism as "legalized greed," and the air we breathe, and it's still outside. We are not thereby baptizing capitalism, but we are saying in this chapter that grace allows us to live with something from which we cannot escape. The grace of God relates to the nature of everyday human experiences.

Since a focus on grace was under an eclipse for centuries before Luther, and his theology removed it from daily life thereafter (Chapter 4), one wonders what Bonhoeffer's "cheap grace" concern was really all about. Perhaps the rapid repetition of "we have sinned against you in thought, word, and deed" in a formal worship confession of sins was so different from his small group experience with students that he had to comment on it, and it was just a comment, a passing reference.

Even when confession is individualized, as in the Roman Catholic tradition, it can veer away from issues relating to where we spend most of our waking hours, i.e., daily work. One such person had stopped going to confession as a younger person when he realized he was not going to quit doing what he confessed.[6] He "confessed" this past to the priest only to receive what amounted to the grace of God. The priest admitted to having the same problem. He even acknowledged that forgiving himself was easy, because he came to like his own sins, and found a reason to do them. Genuine remorse simply vanished.

The priest had the same experience as the Apostle Paul who, in the 1st Century, wrote to his friends in Rome, of all places, that he did not understand his own actions. "I do not do what I want, but I do the very thing I hate" (Romans 7:15).

A CEO may feel this way when he/she has to lay people off. And while forgiveness may sound like cheap grace in covering the pressures of the marketplace, grace is what we need to hear about.

Paul's experience of repeating sins also has marketplace application. In his Second Letter to the Corinthians (12:7) he reveals how three times he asked God to remove what had become a thorn in the flesh. We do not know what it was, but it must have been a besetting sin. However, instead of removing it, God made him aware that grace, not remorse, was a sufficient alternative. Since grace is for sinners, this thorn was probably not a physical malady but a moral one. If so, he ceased "confessing" it and continued doing it under the grace of God. Storeowners can draw a measure of solace from this when they periodically have to charge more than a product is worth to compensate for losses received from other products that do not sell. It might even provide Monday morning incentive to get out of bed.

Conscientious pastors can feel that declaring absolution or forgiveness is itself too easy. They may long to plant their meaning in the minds of their parishioners. However, *longing* is the extent of it. The most anyone can do is to reflect personally on what the words mean—not by proxy—and how the suffering of Jesus on the cross reveals how far God goes to forgive us.

As to the form or reality of contrition, I would only "confess" that it has been fifty years since I shed even one tear over a sin. However, repentance comes from the Greek word *metanoia*, which means "change of mind," not an emotional trip, and here grace for the workplace relates to a timely issue.

JESUS AS CAPITALIST AND SOCIALIST

Two well-known parables reveal opposite views in his mind of low achievers. Both are found in Matthew, the collector of taxes. In Matthew 25:14-30 a 1st Century employer sounds like an investment broker of today. Before going on a trip, he entrusts his servants with different amounts of money, called "talents." To one he gives five, two another two, and to a third he gives one talent. Like good capitalists, the servants with five and two talents trade theirs for more, so when the employer returns, he is pleased. They had invested wisely, (watching the Jerusalem stock market daily). Seeing his boss to be a hard man, the single-talent servant buried his talent to keep it safe, and sure enough, the boss was angry and punished him severely. For some, this parable reinforces their view of the poor as lazy.

In what might be called a socialist story, a vineyard owner goes out at different times during the day to hire people, but at the end of the shift he pays them all the same wage (Matthew 20:1-16). The all-day workers were, of course, miffed at this, as well they might be. Perhaps, however, we would not be reading too much into this parable to suggest that the vineyard owner used the same wage level for all, knowing that they all had similar basic needs.

It would appear from this story that Jesus, alias the vineyard owner, also saw something he considered unfair. It was that people stood around idle because, "No one has hired us." Presumably they were willing to work, but there was a kind of discrimination going on in Century One toward certain members of society. Maybe what bugged the all-day workers was that the vineyard owner made the unemployed equal to them by paying them the same wage.

The conventional interpretation of this parable is to say the all-day workers are the Jews, chosen by God in the beginning, while the ones who are hired late in the day are the Gentiles. Another common interpretation sees the eleventh-hour workers as deathbed converts. Both of these interpretations spiritualize the story.

By ignoring the real life situation, the unemployment setting is by-passed. The vehicle for the story is treated as never existing, when in fact it did. However, whether one interprets it in spiritual or historical terms, the generosity of the vineyard owner remains. What those who worked but one hour received *was* unearned, or unmerited, in comparison to those who worked all day. It was a form of unconditional grace in the workplace.

We can spin the life out of these two parables, but we are still confronted with opposite views of Jesus here. One is almost tempted to say, "Will the real Jesus please stand up."

SOCIAL JUSTICE

Social justice belongs in a chapter on capitalism, but not just because the dynamic of grace is included in the title and contents. There are folks who are strong advocates of social justice of all kinds just for its own sake. However, there are many who cannot advocate social justice because classism gets in the way. As a hangover from the Puritan Work Ethic, the poor are deemed poor because they are lazy. They do not deserve what amounts to a handout. It's the word "deserve" that grace helps overcome. Grace is always undeserved. If it is earned it is not grace. Thus, grace helps many get beyond the cultural barrier to fairness implicit in social justice, and to reach out to those left behind in the journey through life.

One example was my Uncle Ed. He managed a small business, an auto parts store in Rockford, Illinois. They made enough money to make ends meet, but they could have made more if it wasn't for Ed and one of his employees whose IQ was challenged every day. This was back in the 1960's and Ed believed that this person would not get work anywhere else. Besides, he had a wife and children to support. Someone without this handicap could have produced more profit for the store, but rather than fire the man, Ed kept him on for twenty years, paying him his wages. This is an example of grace in the midst of capitalism, and it implies a lot of things, not least of all, generosity and kindness. There are, no doubt, other examples of something like this being done in the world's workplaces.

What bothers those with a social justice conscience is that our brand of capitalism is widening the gap between the rich and the poor, and abandoning many by the side of the road. Standing on the margins of life, they do not feel like they belong to our society. For example, a cleaning woman has to work all year at the minimum wage level to get what the average CEO of a large corporation receives in half a day. Ken Lewis, Bank of America CEO, was paid $20 million in 2003, while that year it laid off 12,500 people, due to a merger with Fleet Bank of Boston.[7] Statistics like this do not rest gently on many minds.

What inspires us, on the other hand, is a man by the name of Aaron Feuerstein. In 1995, a mixture of grace and social justice occurred shortly after a terrible fire destroyed three of four buildings home to the Malden Textile Mills in Lawrence, Massachusetts. Close to 3,000 people were suddenly out of work, but in contrast to corporations that were laying off people, the owner, Mr. Feuerstein, announced, on the very night of the fire, that all of them would remain on the payroll for ninety days. He then commenced rebuilding procedures, noting the economic suffering the citizens of Lawrence had experienced in the 20th Century, and in a subsequent speech to students and friends of the Massachusetts Institute of Technology, he cited the link between religious ethics and business as expressed in the Torah (Deuteronomy 24:14-15). Within four months he had 85% of his people back to work. He lamented the publicity he was receiving for his response to his employees, affirming that they had made the company, and suggesting that praising him only amounted to a sad commentary on the times.

Feuerstein was known for condemning excessive pay to corporate CEOs. They reflected, he said, "an unholy alliance between the moguls of Wall Street and executives with stock options."[8] Now he is also known for his grace and mercy to the people who worked with him to produce a rare kind of clothing fabric.

Unmerited grace, when functioning, does two things simultaneously, which may sound paradoxical. First, even though we participate everyday in the capitalistic economic system, we are forgiven for this bow to avarice. And second, understanding unearned grace gives us a greater concern, not a lesser one, for others in our society who are not yet included in the benefits of decent incomes.

AN EASTER SUNDAY CONVERSATION

Five family members at the table were asked these questions as we awaited dessert: Do management people where you work ever get upset, or angry? How about those lower on the corporate ladder? If so, what is done to deal with the conflict? Does forgiveness ever happen? Responses follow:

Anger in higher corporate echelons comes from unwelcome surprises, and from plans that have not been carried out. Those at lower levels become most upset when reading in the paper what the CEO makes.

Management will place the expectations higher, knowing they cannot be reached, but that way people work harder to accomplish things.

If a problem arises, the cause is first explored by middle management, and if it persists, they are often blamed for the failure. Those in the middle fear those above them, and those below fear those in the middle.

Heads of schools expect teachers to do what they are hired to do— to meet pedagogical expectations. If they do not, it is brought to their attention in performance evaluations.

Forgiveness happens on different levels. Small slights and misunderstandings between teachers are handled that way all the time, without even saying anything about it. For really big mistakes, I don't know.

Labor relations personnel are brought in to help negotiate the conflict where I work. These include lawyers well versed in corporate law, and union stewards.

When it comes to a conflict of views between top management levels and workers, top-level people rule. They decide what to do.

Aren't W. Edwards Deming's ideas acceptable anymore?

What we have in the above workplaces are pyramids supported by law and power. It is believed necessary to make the organization run smoothly. The same is true in religious organizations. There is no grace at the top of the pyramids in either the church or the workplace.

Early in this chapter we pointed out how Bonhoeffer went too far in suggesting that it is wrong to promise forgiveness to those who do not have an acute awareness of sin or contrition. Lack of an awareness of grace forces us to transfer awareness of our own failure to somebody else. An angry God does not inspire self-honesty, but a kindly one can. It even prompts an employer to keep people on the payroll for months after a catastrophe has destroyed their place of work.

CONVERSATION STARTERS

FOR CHAPTER 9

◇? If God forgives a person for making profit a lifelong pursuit, is it cheap grace?

◇? How does grace relate to a CEO who makes $20 million in the same year the company lays off 12,000?

◇? Is grace costly for us today?

◇? Is remorse possible to measure, or must we take someone's word for it?

◇? How does God's forgiveness of repetitious sins provide hope for those working in our capitalistic system?

◇? How do you assess the difference in the two parables of Jesus?

◇? In your words, how would you connect grace and social justice?

"Paul Johnson has effectively drawn upon many relevant religious sources and scores of personal experiences as a Pastor to define Grace. The issue that he joins is grace in the Workplace. This book gives the reader much to consider in reaching a conclusion.

His understanding of people in the workplace and his clarification of grace serve as important reference points to help the reader. The challenge has been made and the tools provided. All that is needed is acceptance.

A 'must read' for management."

**Robert Kondracki, former Principal at
Southeastern Massachusetts Vocational Technical School**

WHAT UNCONDITIONAL GRACE IMPLIES

10

DEPENDING ON WHO ONE asks, unconditional grace could be foolishness to some or the gift of God to others. To the first group it smacks of looking the other way, or letting someone get away with murder. To the second group it is the paradigm of the New Testament

Monday morning incentive for grace in the workplace can come from Sunday morning grace-oriented sermons. In this book, we focus on ways to import grace into the pulpit. However, it would increase rapport if each time the pastor candidly acknowledged that the goal is toward grace becoming a *corporate foundational policy*. Forums where laypersons help relate grace to workplace problems could supplement these sermons.

A NON-JUDGMENTAL PRESENCE

The child Isaiah (9:6) said would one day be born on earth and later be called "Mighty God," grew to manhood in Nazareth of Galilee, without the local citizens having a clue as to his identity. A framework of reality fills in the threadbare Gospel accounts of what happened during those years. They don't say Jesus was ever a carpenter, but it doesn't make sense to assume that he stood around watching Joseph work, or that he had a well-paying job in a nearby city.

We can assume that for years Jesus labored, first as a wood worker's apprentice, and then, presumably when Joseph died, he continued the trade. His conversation must have been mostly job related. Thus, when he spoke in the local synagogue, at the age of thirty, about his reason for being born, the reaction was "Is not this Joseph's son?" They were accustomed to hearing him talk shop, not vocational destiny.

When Jesus needed a piece of wood, he had to cut, trim, and fit it carefully. That he merely pulled a shorter one to the desired length is too sleight of hand. Had this ever happened, it would have been included in the New Testament.[1] On the other hand, a carpenter who blended in with the other citizens as if he were just another peasant would not stand out. All week he wore work clothes, as is true in the trades today.

Had Jesus quoted Scripture in his daily conversation, his announcement in the synagogue would have seemed normal, not unexpected. As it was, nobody thought of him as any more religious than anyone else. Yet, because of who he was, his relationship was a daily sharing of theistic grace. In his quiet acceptance of flawed humanity, we find divine magnanimity at work, grace for Jesus' earthly workplace. It would seem fair to conclude that he knew the folks in Nazareth without trying to change them. God's unconditional presence was visibly with them for thirty years, but unknown as such.

Thus, when at the age of thirty Jesus took up his brief public ministry, he reveals something of Nazareth. His understanding of God did not hit him or anyone else like a lightning bolt from the sky. It grew and matured slowly in a small town. His message is pitched toward the poor because he came from those roots.

One of these thirty-year insights is not insisting on contrition as a precondition for forgiveness. This is why Jesus tells Peter to forgive "seventy times seven." This is why he does not ask Peter to first examine the recipients to detect if they are sufficiently contrite to receive it. Moreover, in anticipation, when Jesus does not have the father of the Prodigal Son call for a confession from his errant prodigy, he is not abusing the gift of grace; he is applying it.

While multiplying the two numbers *seven* and *seventy* would be a symbolic movement in the direction of infinity, even to forgive the same person 490 times would include many of the same infractions, among which could be the "seven deadly sins." It is a tacit recognition on Jesus' part of the propensity for repeated offenses. The implication is that forgiveness is unconditional, and the ability to repeatedly grant it is divine forbearance. And it would seem apropos to suggest that this applies to corporate "sinners" such as Martha Stewart, not just holy people who stumble on their stairway to heaven.

Nowhere in the Gospels does forgiveness without either confession or contrition speak to us more than from the parable of the Prodigal Son, for here we do not rely on implication. Unconditional grace is built into the story. We do not know if the younger son is sorry for having squandered his inheritance. He might have been, or he might have been so desperate he would do anything to get food in his belly and a roof over his head. Either way, it seems reasonable to assume he thought his father would be angry and that having a confession in mind might come in handy. However, the father runs to his son and hugs him before he even gets the words out. As for overt remorse, it is conspicuous only by its absence.

By implication, we could assert from the parable that to this son, the father's behavior must have been a complete surprise. The son could have expected him to say, "Show me the money!" or to ask "Where have you been?" Parents can raise the latter query when children come home an hour later than expected, let alone years later. However, there is no interrogation, no third degree. Instead, there is only an embrace from a father whose gladness of heart illuminates the household. Surely this would be an example of what has been labeled "cheap grace." Putting the best robe on him would be extravagance—mercy gone awry. Uncondtional grace is cheap until we take Jesus use of it into account. However, while contrition may be good for the soul and confession therapeutic for the mind, the focus of this parable is on the response of the "father," who is analogous to God.

INDISPENSABLE TO THE KERYGMA

To hear good news in the Gospel books it is not enough to focus on the death and resurrection the way Matthew, Mark, Luke, and John do. Along with the "kerygma" there must also be unconditional grace. This is what makes the Good News good.

For the women disciples at the scene of the crucifixion, it was enough to learn that Jesus was no longer in the tomb, but for the male disciples who fled the scene it took more than that. It required knowledge that Jesus did not hold their cowardice against them. This he provided in his appearances.

In the biblical story, it is debatable which was the worse "sin," the betrayal by Judas or the denial by Simon Peter. Judas' was the more deceptive, Peter's the more blatant. Both of them were stricken with guilt, but had Judas been present to meet Jesus after the resurrection, it is reasonable to believe that the amnesty Jesus visited upon his core group of AWOL male friends, would have included Judas also.

The words "Peace be with you" and "Fear not" were filled with redemption for the deserters when Jesus uttered them in their post-Easter hiding place. Although neither the word *grace* nor the word *forgiveness* were spoken, they were implicit in the peace. Indeed, they were present in his seeking the disciples out. It was as if he wanted them to know there were no hard feelings—anger, wrath, or vengeance—on his part. For Peter, the resurrection was cause for fear, until he looked into the eyes of Christ and saw kindness.

For many workplace denizens, a similar dynamic would occur were a CEO to visit a small group without chastising them for making a mistake in some decision. Seeing him, hearing him, would be like "Fear not, I bring you peace."

Furthermore, when it comes to the four Gospels, there is enough law and warning in them to discourage even the staunchest Pharisee. Without the good news of grace in some of Jesus' parables and in the theology of Paul, it is difficult to say they are the conveyers of glad tidings, though Christendom has glibly spoken of them in that light for a long time. Jesus needs Paul just as much as Paul needs Jesus. And the grace of God speaks through both of them.

CASTS OUT FEAR OF PUNISHMENT

The reference in Chapter 2 to corporations that allow small groups of workers to make decisions without fear of reprisal deserves commentary here. It seems reasonable to suggest that for management to trust the labor force in this way would increase the morale of the workers, and it would allow workers closest to the problem, if that is what they are resolving, to deal with it, thereby building their confidence.

What may be less apparent is the extent to which such a policy is the fulfillment of the biblical insight that perfect love casts out the fear of punishment. When the threat of reprisal for mistakes is removed, workers can also trust management. Indeed, when management makes mistakes, workers who have been treated to this trust in small groups would be more understanding and forgiving of those above them on the corporate ladder.

It should be acknowledged that in workplace decision groups there is a built-in peer pressure that would deter some from slacking off. However, words from fellow workers, it would seem, would be more effective and laced with more understanding than having to appear before a management person.

The words in John's letter—"Perfect love casts out fear, for fear has to do with punishment" (1 John 4:16-18)—could not be clearer. The perfect love that John describes is that of God. It is a powerful theme, one that fits in with the words of Jesus: "Be ye perfect as your Heavenly Father is perfect." It is a Mt. Everest type of passage, unparalleled in any other religion. And it is another way of describing the unconditionality of grace. It is also a way of describing God as the center of the weekday world.

Down in the valley, the above is written off as being soft on sin. Our judicial system is steeped in punitivity, as is the threat implicit in performance reviews. We speak of a prison as a house of correction but it is, primarily, a warehouse where one pays his or her debt to that abstraction called society. In America, punishment is an institution; grace an occasion. This, too often, includes the church.

Due to ecclesiastical structure and moralistic law, unconditional grace is rarely seen even in the organization commissioned to share it—the church. It is a policy in the group with which I am affiliated, for example, to remove from the ministry pastors who are accused of sexual affairs. A double standard ensues, for lay members are not similarly removed from the roster. What this does is undermine the trust in divine grace and trust in the hierarchy. Some laypersons wonder what chance they have as laypersons to received God's grace, if pastors are exempt from it.[2]

In the context of the Prodigal Son parable, it should be noted that for *some* the real prodigal is the father. His forgiveness becomes foolhardy when the son's debauchery is taken seriously. Had he really cared for his son, he would have wrung the contrition out of him. And if there was none, then the next best thing would be reparations. The son must pay for his sins. Keep scolding him until his morals improve. Later he *might* appreciate his father's goodwill, but not until.

In the story, on the other hand, we are reminded that the father is happy that his son is back home. It's as if life itself has been punishment enough. Wesley Shader, in his book *Yeshua's Diary*, has Jesus reflect as follows:

> The longer I am in the flesh, the more restless I become with the limitations and restrictions imposed by such an existence. My candid judgment is that men (and women) deserve far more credit than is generally given them for participating in the life of this world. To be a dying member of a dying humanity—and to know that this is the case—is weight enough to bear.[3]

For those who would press for repentance, it is available, of course, in the Gospels and in the thinking of Jesus, e.g., the parable about the two men who went into the temple to pray. A 1ˢᵗ Century IRS official prays: "Have mercy upon me, Lord, for I am a sinner," whereas the other man thanked God that he was not like those whose presence he regarded as a kind of contamination (Luke 18:9-14). However, this was a story designed to reach out to the Pharisees, for whom truth would have to be experienced before grace could mean anything in this life.

Unconditional grace does not overlook the largest barrier to Jesus' public ministry—religious authority personified in most Pharisees. His teachings about forgiveness are a personal affront to them; their pride and self-righteousness make others feel sinful by comparison. They probably did not know they did this to people, but Jesus knew. So ingrained was their way of functioning as human beings, they probably regarded their oppressive behavior as normal. That Jesus would lock horns with them was inevitable.

Telling them they were pious only on the outside must have been a shock. Yet, in the telling, Jesus is performing a ministry. As Bonhoeffer observes in *Life Together*, it is to our advantage to become disillusioned with our own goodness, for then we may begin to appreciate the grace of God.[4] By deflating their self-image, Jesus is paving the way for them at some point in this life, or in the next, to have an experience of the Eternal Word, based on unearnable mercy.

GRACE IS TRUMP

There are those in the pews and in the workplace who will draw encouragement from these three words. Our first hint of this hope comes when Jesus said that among men born of women there was none greater than John the Baptist (Matthew 11:11). He was the prophet of doom. Law and wrath exude from his pores. Yet, said Jesus, one who is least in the kingdom of heaven is greater than John.

John was an Ace of Spades, but Hearts were trump.

In Chapter 1 of his Letter to the Romans, Paul uncharacteristically places all who covet, harbor malice, gossip, are haughty, boastful, or disobedient to parents, under the wrath of God. Then, in the very next chapter, he observes how it is the "kindness of God" that leads to repentance. "Kindness" emerges as an insight that suddenly occurs to him. Whatever, it relates to his subsequent emphasis on grace.

Paul's references to both law and gospel are used in some theological schools to instruct future pastors to keep a balance between the two. However, Paul does not treat them as equals.

In two places, Paul's distinction between law and grace reaches a definitive level. One is when he writes to the Ephesians (2:14-16) how the cross of Christ has broken down the dividing wall of hostility between Jews and Gentiles. Jesus has abolished the law, with its commandments and ordinances, that he might create in himself one new humanity in place of the two, thus making peace. Theologians who castigate preachers for "relaxing the demands of the law," have not given a passage like this its full weight.

Recall that moment when Rene McPherson, new CEO of the Dana Corporation, carried in an armful of corporation rules and after discerning that the chairman of the Board had not read them, dumped them all in the circular file and substituted one sheet on which company guidelines placed people ahead of rules (Chapter 2).

In Paul's second letter to the Corinthians, he describes the Mosaic law as having no splendor *at all* because of the splendor of grace that surpasses it. It is the difference between the sun and the moon. The passage is as follows:

> Now if the dispensation of death, carved in letter on stone [the Ten Commandments], came with such splendor that the Israelites could not look on Moses' face because of it brightness, fading as this was, will not the dispensation of the Spirit be attended with

greater splendor? For if there was splendor in the dispensation of condemnation, the dispensation of righteousness [grace and forgiveness] must exceed it in splendor. **Indeed, in this case what once had splendor has come to have no splendor at all, because of the splendor that surpasses it.** (Second Corinthians 3:7-10)

In these verses, Paul is dealing with the logical conclusion to which the dichotomy between law and grace leads. The first condemns, the second redeems. Since God cannot help being God, both the demands of law and the forgiveness of sin are in God's nature. However, it is significant that the same religion that demands perfection is the one that lifts up the unconditional nature of grace. Since perfection is beyond us, grace is our hope. That grace is greater than law is implicit in their opposite effects. As to the demands of the law, grace simply transcends them.

GENERAL AMNESTY

In our human shortsightedness we imagine divine grace to be finite. But the moment comes when we see and realize that grace is infinite. Grace, my friends, demands nothing from us but that we shall await it with confidence and acknowledge it in gratitude. Grace . . . makes no conditions and singles out none of us in particular; grace takes us all to its bosom and proclaims general amnesty.[5]

This is how a retired French general describes unconditional grace, for which his battlefield experience forms the backdrop. He is attending a dinner in honor of the deceased founder of a tiny cultlike Lutheran group, being held together by his two daughters in a village on a Norwegian fjord.

This kind of grace appears throughout the book and movie, *Babette's Feast*. Babette was a famous chef in Paris who has to flee during the French Revolution, but she doesn't reveal her culinary credentials. Grace shows up when, after agreeing to work for two sisters, she patiently accepts their instructions on how to prepare their daily menu—boiled codfish and bread soup. A further hint occurs when she also improves its taste.

Grace surfaces when, after winning a French lottery, Babette asks if she can serve a dinner in honor of the group's founder. Having been brought up to believe that all pleasure is sinful, the sisters are appalled at the parade of food imported for the event. They see the wine as the "Devil's brew." Fearing they may have erred, they confess it to the little group, who agree to not say a word about the meal, while eating it as if they "never had a sense of taste." By *pretending* not to enjoy it, they assume they will not tarnish the religious image of the founder of their little colony. The general, who is a guest, is dumfounded when, after they taste the food, the only words he hears are "Isn't it a nice day?"

Undeserved grace emerges when Babette serves up a gourmet's delight without receiving a word of thanks for it from the group. The two sisters receive unconditional grace when she informs them that all her lottery money was used to pay for the food, and then asks them if she can continue working for them.

It is essential, however, to underscore how this grace came through a kitchen, from a *workplace*, not from the church place. It lets us say the workplace is an *extension* of the church place. Grace came as God's unconditional mercy, quietly trumping the legalistic piety of law through the person and artistry of a gourmet cook. However, it is doubtful anyone but the military guest realized what God was doing among them.

* * *

General amnesty is a benevolent idea, but it raises one final issue—when do we receive or experience it? There are many for whom grace is not a part of faith. How about them? In fact, most folks die without gaining an awareness of it. Is there post-mortem mercy? The following story touches upon an answer.

A businessman found himself outside the Pearly Gates. He knocked and waited. St. Peter came to the door and the man said, "I would like to enter," to which St. Peter replied, "To do that you will need 1,000 points."

The man wasn't prepared for this, so he noted what he thought St. Peter would want to hear: "I've gone to church all my life."

"That's worth one point," the keeper of the gate informed him, much to the man's chagrin.

"I've worked hard in the church," the man responded, assuming that was what the sainted fisherman was looking for.

"One point," answered St. Peter.

At this the businessman began to worry. He noted how he had been the husband of one wife, had never had an affair, and, as if he had suddenly remembered what would surely count, he added, "We brought our children up in the church." One point for each of those was all he could muster. Panic set in and he trotted out what amounted to his last desperate hope. "I've read the Bible from cover to cover."

"One point," observed St. Peter.

"Heavens," cried the businessman, "The only way you can get in here is by the grace of God."

"One thousand points," exclaimed the old salt, with a twinkle in his eye.

The man had heard about the grace of God, but the meaning had escaped him. As his law-like answers reveal, grace had no connection with his daily work. They were all churchy, so he had to wait until death to experience it. The bottom line is that *no one* is left behind.

CONVERSATION STARTERS

FOR CHAPTER 10

Would unmerited grace or forgiveness for "religious sins" be relevant or applicable to corporation errors?

Why was mercy not shown to someone like Martha Stewart?

Do you know of any companies who kept someone on the work roster who was handicapped in some way?

Was the mellowing of the spirit of the little flock due to the wine or unconditional grace? If the wine, was it the "Devil's brew"?

THE PULPIT WORKPLACE

11

THE TIME HAS COME to lift up topics and texts from this book that could be used in the pulpit to tailor make the *Lectionary to Grace for the Workplace*, and inspire Monday morning incentive. Readers will have different responses to, and will vary in their use of, this book, and that is most in keeping with the grace that frees us to do what we want or nothing at all. Most preachers will agree, however, that they work more then twenty minutes on a sermon. That barely covers the delivery time. Preparation time is considerably longer.

Where a reader would like to incorporate the ideas in this book to the pulpit/pew setting, there would be value in involving a group of lay persons in the planning stage, perhaps meeting at a restaurant for lunch, so the setting confirms that this is not business as usual.

It would be important to make sure that what is utilized does not turn grace for the workplace into another law. The tone of the material that makes it into the pulpit needs to be one of declaration not an order from above, another bar on which we chin ourselves, or just another law to obey. We will try to get into that in what follows. The bulleted items are those that would be possible pulpit material, with the chapters and their relevant paragraphs as further background.

THE INTRODUCTION PHASE

If I were starting off with this subject in a congregation, I would move slowly but try to arouse some curiosity at the same time. One avenue toward this end would be to employ the "Bell Ringing" experiment described in Chapter 3. I waited close to three months to assure spontaneity, but looking back, I do not think it would have been necessary to wait that long. After *one* month the congregation stopped thinking about the bell. Both pulpit and pew would, however, benefit from knowing that sermon thoughts find their way into lay minds during the pulpit delivery.

📖 To introduce the notion of the pulpit relating to the workplace, there would be value in using the parable-based "Prologue," perhaps done in a skit form, and following that up with material from the "Memo to the CEO." The Prologue is very short, but having a small table in the front of the church with four or five chairs around, it would be an appropriate chancel drama. Then the pastor could share the thoughts from the "Memo," along with any of his or her own that it prompts. The theological item from Bonhoeffer—God is at the center of the weekday world—would be a natural connection with folks who spend all their time there. A biblical text might be Matthew 28:20, "I am with you always."

📖 Another consideration, with language from the workplace and content from the church, might be "The Boss and the Foreman" discussion of reasons for the atonement. It uses contrast to make clear what grace means. This would also be a subject an adult education group might get into. Most parishioners will realize that what went on between God and Jesus on the cross is presented in a semi-parable form. However, what may be news to many laypersons are the various theories of the atonement. In the 1950s, professors of systematic theology presented thirteen theories of what happened between God and Jesus on the cross as if they were *all* valid. For me, it was a mind blower to hear there were thirteen, but it was years before fundamentalism joined four of them in one group, focused on God's wrath, leaving God's mercy to emerge as an opposite approach.

ON-GOING OPTIONS

Chapter 7, "Under New Management," is a practical way of letting folks in the pews know sermons are trying to relate to the workplace. It's a frequent sign hanging in front of a place of business, and it serves as a follow-through from the previous "Boss and Foreman" chapter. The chapter has a homiletical division of three parts, but that would be too much for one sermon. One part per sermon might be enough exposure at a time.

📖 The first section, headed "Expansion," you may recall, deals with decision making. The illustrations are such that management persons in the audience are not going to be offended by them, even if they are more accustomed to traditional management styles. A text that relates well to the sharing of authority and responsibility is Matthew 20:25 where Jesus urges his followers to think of themselves as brothers and sisters in relation to each other, rather than lording it over others "as the Gentiles do." Even though a pew sitter may not have this sharing of decision-making opportunity where he or she works, a view of work is being developed here, and the overall picture might stimulate some coffee-hour conversation.

📖 The next section in this chapter is "Motivation." It presents logic from Scripture and the dictionary that demonstrates how mercy is more motivating than wrath when it comes to inaugurating new management ideas. The section has many biblical texts, and makes a case for mercy in the Hebrew scripture being the precursor for grace in the Christian scripture. Another word for mercy is "compassion" or even "understanding," which may be easier for workers to relate to the workplace, but the chapter presents them as all cut from the same cloth.

📖 "Interpretation," the last section in Chapter 7, attempts to reconcile the opposites of wrath and mercy appearing in the Bible. Although the case for human projection is one source for wrath, a reflection of telling someone to "go to hell," another explanation is that mercy was a divine breakthrough in the Hebrew scripture's emphasis on wrath. The Old and New Testaments are not presented as opposites here, but wrath and mercy are.

Chapter 8, "Grace in Three Work Areas," provides glimpses of grace already at work, suggesting that God is at the center of the workforce week.

📖 Luther's location of "Moses and the law books" on earth, and grace in heaven, splits the psyche of parishioners who are in the legal professions, law enforcement, or the military. A sermon on the material in this section on the police department, even though it gains its impetus from Japan, allows workers in these fields to realize there is at least a potential dimension to grace, even in their work.

📖 "Corporations" lifts up the way the workplace democracy movement has grace-filled overtones. Anecdotal illustrations include the Dana Corporation (Chapter 2), Starbucks, and Southwest Airlines.

📖 Parishioners who are into sports, and many are, would appreciate the illustrations of grace at work in athletics, not the kind that allows for graceful movement but the biblical kind. One sermon on sports out of fifty-two should not offend anti-jocks, especially when it extends this dimension of faith to such a large part of our culture. Moreover, it will broaden the scope of grace in the thoughts patterns of the workforce.

Chapter 9 on **"Grace and Capitalism,"** might at first seem frightening, and that in itself is a curious phenomenon. Being our economic system, capitalism is the corporate engine that drives us to work, though some parishioners may be out of work for one reason or another. If presented in the context of the workplace, grace can encourage church folks to deal with issues capitalism raises, and has raised throughout their lives, but have been kept in a closet.

📖 It is natural to tie in the lifelong forgiveness of God, the focus on profit-making in the workplace, and the concept of "cheap grace" coined by Bonhoeffer. The irony here is that despite the satisfaction one derives from making a good profit, without having heard a word against it in church, one can wonder how God feels about this devotion to business and industry. The next section "The Past is Prologue Once More," could be drawn from to show how the issue has been around for a long time. Cheap grace very much needs to be rethought, and this context lets it happen with a practical application.

📖 The juxtaposing of the parables of the vineyard owner (paying all the same) and the employer who expected returns on his one-, two-, and five-talent investments will stimulate the workplace in the pews in a fresh way. Preaching on these parables separately and a year apart never allows this to happen, but it's there, nonetheless. Most of us do not deal with it, though some preachers may have already done so. Our precedent of spiritualizing the equal payment parable and capitalizing the talent parable, may have helped us keep them distinct, but we still have to cope with the question of which parable is more true to the grace of God.

📖 Having opened up consideration of our capitalistic system and its relation to grace, another natural follow-through is to relate grace to social justice, as this chapter does. The inequity should be cited, if this is used, but the positive illustrations of social justice in small and large businesses are the inspiration for this issue. Both

108 ◇ *Grace for the Workplace*

entrepreneurs demonstrated grace and social justice joined together.

Chapter 10, "What Unconditional Grace Implies," gets at the heart of it, and could provide sermon content for a series all in itself.

📖 It is conventional practice to follow lectionary selections, which means leapfrogging from the birth of Jesus to his three-year ministry, with perhaps a stop off at the temple. This leaves the thirty years in Nazareth as a carpenter to rest uncomfortably in the silent zone of the great unsaid, subject to occasional questions, but little commentary. In the context of grace for the workplace, we must include it. Jesus' thirty years in the workplace as a tradesman is a most plausible prelude to some of his teachings that do not place importance on confession or contrition, but circumvent them. Unconditional grace is cheap until we bring Jesus' own use of it into account. This allows two contacts with rethinking cheap grace, but it might not hurt to repeat it in a year or so.

📖 The section "Grace is Trump" uses an allusion to a card term which allows us to relate grace to the law as Paul does in several of his letters. It would allow the pastor to reinforce Paul's focus on grace, in contrast to law, and make sermonic use of the Letters in a gospel orientation. To borrow a thought from that section, grace does not relax the law, it transcends it, so there is no danger of antinomian heresy here.

📖 For a homiletical change of pace, describing the book and film, *Babette's Feast*, in this section on "General Amnesty" would allow an insight on unconditional grace to surface in a story context all by itself, with some commentary at the end. As a cook, Babette knows what work is, but that does not prevent her from illustrating, albeit unwittingly, the content of grace in a most intriguing manner. A preacher could have fun with this one.

MANY PACKAGES, ONE GIFT

Each branch of the Christian family tree has inherited the same gift of grace, but there is a tendency for attention to the package to distract from it. Whether wrappings or trappings, the effects are similar. We have one gift but many packages.

Meanings attached to colors of clergy vestments, plus shapes and locations of holy furniture, can overshadow the focal point on grace. Secondary beliefs harden into identities for telling members of the family apart.

In the 16th Century, Martin Luther became known for what we might call a hat trick, or triple priorities. These were faith alone, scripture alone, and grace alone. In effect, only one of these deserves that distinction. Only grace can carry the weight placed upon it—by the other two.

A writer and assessor of Christianity from the 19th Century, Ludwig Feuerbach once said that faith divides but love unites.[3] When he saw each Christian denomination parading its identity beliefs as *the* correct package, it seemed to him that "faith" was a divisive force, whereas love had the opposite effect, if given the chance to function.

When we relate Feuerbach's insight to the three "alones," we see that faith is never alone, nor is scripture. These are always in some historical context. Faith varies with the group that is defining it, and scripture has as many interpretations as there are interpreters. Both faith and scripture, therefore, point to human elements. And even when we lift up "grace" we have to be careful.

Luther's experience of unconditional grace was the product of a unique mix of historical circumstances that have not been replicated anywhere in any century since then. He lived in deeply superstitious times. A fear of God was exacerbated by practices in the Catholic Church and by Luther's own personality. He tried to please God by whipping himself, or by recalling some sin he must not have confessed, but he found no peace. He assumed God was angry with him for something. Nevertheless, God related to him, using the Letters of Paul as a catalyst for grace. Remove these historical circumstances, however, and people today can understand grace, but we cannot experience it the way Luther did.

Nonetheless, in reality there is only one belief that points to salvation for anybody, and that belief is grace alone, or general amnesty. It is synonymous with the perfect love that casts out the fear of punishment, as described in John's First Letter (4:16-18). Whether called unconditional, unmerited grace or perfect love, it is the nature of God, not human nature, to be this way. It transcends all packages.

By its very definition, grace alone points to God. When grace is joined with the word "alone" or the term "unconditional," then God is the only referent. The kind of love Paul says bears all things and endures all things is only possible for the Creator. Only God is able to be unconditionally gracious all the time.

That is also why grace is big enough to unite all the denominations in Christendom. In a sense, grace eliminates the need for ecumenism, for it is something we already have in God. It only needs to be recognized as such.

EPILOGUE

THOSE WHO ENJOY MYSTERY stories will recall how some authors at the end of their tales have an epilogue to tell readers what happened to the key characters several fictional years later. Since this book is technically not a story, there are no characters to do that with, but there is one character, the author, and I would like to let the reader in on several issues encountered in writing on this subject that required some unusual persistence.

WORKPLACE IN THE PEWS

One of these areas was working with the realization that every Sabbath/Sunday the workplace is seated in the pews. It was as if they were hiding in plain sight, or perhaps it was that other issues kept intruding themselves into my thoughts when I tried to focus on both labor and management sitting there week after week.

Part of this internal response was the way my mind was programmed to prepare sermons. It was a kind of formula that included first the exegesis of a text, i.e. what it meant to those who first wrote it or read it, and then application to the present day world. I found that as the years went by, I spent more time trying to understand the text, so that there wasn't a lot of time left for application. By application, I mean illustrating something from daily life, and the weird part was that where people spent the best part of their daytime hours was not included in my understanding of "daily life." It was as if the laity left home and just disappeared for eight hours. In any event, my "illustrations" never entered the workplace, and the "daily life" was often mine.

I was writing a book that sought to enter a realm I did not really know. No wonder my editor had to point my nose in the right direction, to sniff out the issues at times, lest I venture too far into the esoteric land of theology in some chapters and leave the lay folks behind in the process. I greatly appreciated her reminding me of this from time to time, and then reading it over carefully to see if I had made my point. That's one reason editors are invaluable.

Another way of saying this is that the congregation's weekday location was, for me, a case of "out of sight, out of mind." I had relationships with parishioners through "pastoral acts" when I was serving as a pastor. I met with them for weddings and funerals and sometimes baptisms, or as someone has called it, I hatched, matched, and dispatched them. As for seeing them in their place of work, that happened on occasion but it did not really make it into the pulpit.

I recall a church secretary saying her father was inviting me to visit him where he worked, a foundry at the Fafner Bearing Company in New Britain, Connecticut. It was primarily a visual experience. He would stand facing the open furnace door with a fire raging a few feet away, and insert and remove iron ingots. His front side was hot, his backside cold. I supposed I could have used that as a new way of picturing hell and heaven, or something, but I had left that medieval image behind.

I worked other "secular" jobs in summers during college years, and delivered mail over Christmas vacation, but these, too, were visually-oriented experiences. I learned nothing about labor/management relationships, or the demands lay workers were under, and what dumfounds me is that when I met with the foundry worker, I didn't ask him any questions that might have led to my learning something. By way of excuse, I think I was awestruck by the conditions under which he earned his living.

I think one other thing may have tugged at my mind on the "workplace in the pews" theme. It was having been made aware by Merton P. Strommen, a researcher out of Minneapolis, that two-thirds of the folks in the pews had a law orientation to "Christianity." All Lutheran clergy received a complimentary copy of his book, *A Study of Generations*, in 1972. One of his findings was that the majority of those sitting in the pews believed the essence of the Gospel was "God's rules for right living." Hearing of this in the context of Martin Luther and his publicized focus on *grace alone* was disconcerting. What was going on here? And why?

In a sense, I should have been able to put this together, for there was a weekly clue sermon listeners were giving me. At the door, the most response I received from anyone was "Good morning, pastor." It came through to me as if they had not heard what I had spent hours preparing. In my first parish, I just assumed this was "church work," but as the years rolled by, it got to me. I recall during the years of the Vietnam War how this hit me with enough impact to force my resignation from that parish and go back to school to learn more about the pulpit/pew relationship. I would, at times, say something about the war in a sermon, but it produced no comment at the door. Surely they must have heard and read the same news I did. It was amazing!

CONTRASTING LAW AND GRACE

This was the second theme that I had to wrestle with in this book. Actually, it was a dominant one, but it was not easy because other factors were at work in my mind. I had been trained in theological school to think of law and gospel as created equal. I was to think of a healthy tension existing between the two, one that kept them in balance. If I tipped too far to one side or the other, I was led to think this was some kind of homiletical heresy. There was even the view espoused that first the preacher had to hit the people over the head with the law, as it were, and then he could lay on the healing balm of grace. It was a one-two punch. I was to play the bad cop, good cop game.

Looking back on this seminary indoctrination, I wonder how this was received by pew sitters who were under the law gun five days a week, and who had to face the demands of their work with periodic performance reviews thrown in to keep their toes to the line. I recall visiting a Veteran's hospital when touring with a seminary choir, and being told by the chaplain that one thing his "parishioners" did not need to hear was law. They were already loaded with guilt feelings from the war. What they needed was grace, over and over again, just to keep their heads above water. The workplace is a kind of war, especially where competition is raging away.

I would underscore here the impact on me of two Lutheran theologians, Martin Luther and Dietrich Bonhoeffer. While Luther wrote about "grace alone" and believed it for himself, in his Commentary on Galatians he plants a landmine when he writes that grace only fits in when one is thinking about sin, heaven, or Christ, whereas, in this life what counts are Moses and the law books. He wasn't so much lamenting this as encouraging it.

Bonhoeffer's contribution to this quandary over grace was to refer to it as "cheap" as we considered in a section in Chapter 9 on "Grace and Capitalism." If anyone did actually *hear* my sermons it must have sounded as if I were blaming them for making grace cheap, but after a while I just stopped talking about grace. After all, if Bonhoeffer, whom I greatly admired, said that grace was cheap, who was I to argue? It was not the reason parishioners, i.e. the workforce in the pews, were law oriented, but sidelining grace surely did not help any.

And last but not least in this law/grace theme, is the Lectionary, the list of assigned texts for Sunday sermons. I had long thought there were a lot of them that emphasized law, encouraging exhortation and admonishment, but not until 2004 did I realize how true this was. I read all the Gospel selections for that year and even though I noted this in Chapter 1, it is crucial enough to warrant a repeat here; law outnumbers grace texts by five to one. Forty percent of the time, if the preacher is going to be true to the text, sermons are going to have a load of law in them. In this book I have suggested that we need to import more grace into the pulpit, whether it is officially sanctioned by the theological powers that be or not.

The church has little chance of declaring grace, even if it wants to, providing it follows the assigned texts. Indeed, two of the five Gospel texts that touch on grace, either implicitly or explicitly, come during the summer months, when many regulars are on vacation.

GOD IN THE WORKPLACE

This is the final theme that I found hard to keep in mind in this book. Some readers will recall how it was Bonhoeffer again, this time in his book on *Ethics,* who declared that God was not holed up in church all week, but that the center of His activity from Monday through Saturday was in the world, alias "the workplace." God was at work in the secular world all week long. It was a provocative idea, but what to do with it?

Part of the problem was that I have not worked "in the world," in this context. I did during seminary days, but that was a while back, and I was not even remotely considering God's relationship to the workplace then. Even with full-time workplace people in the pews at my first two parishes, I did not think of it. Then, too, I think this was also hard for me to contemplate because of the effect of associating God with the church place. It was as if God was wearing a robe, surplice, alb, and stole, not just me. As I reflect on it, it was amazing that I thought of God wearing any clothes, but this was religion and religion was God's garment.

What helped was W. Edwards Deming, the guru of workplace democracy some years ago. His thoughts about making daily work a better experience were secular versions of biblical dynamics, especially unconditional grace. Grace became the footprints to look for in the secular world for this God that made it his center of concern during the weekday.

Thank you, for sharing these themes with me through reading.

"This thoughtful and practical guide is a 'must read' for pastors, worship leaders, teachers, seminary faculty, seminarians and all who shape the direction of the church. This book is important because it points us back to the heart of the gospel. Grace is God's heart. If God is in our hearts, He is with us in our workplaces.

Respecting all employees, giving them a voice in the decisions that affect their work is not only good business, it is an act of grace. The church can become more relevant in society by fostering grace, encouraging parishioners to build grace into managerial relationships. I have worked in many places and know firsthand how wonderful it is to experience grace in the workplace.

Chapter 6, 'The Boss and the Foreman', made the shift in understanding God's grace quite effectively. Forums to discuss grace using this chapter as a guide for reflection would be very effective in both understanding grace and translating it to the workplace. The power of grace came through so clearly in the contrasting scenarios. Well done!

This book reminds us that we need to open the doors of the church and our hearts and let grace work through us. Thank you for your prod to spread the good news in every part of our lives."

Lauren J. Holm, RN, MSN Staff Specialist
Massachusetts General Hospital

"Have you ever been struck by the presence or seeming absence of God at work? Are work and church one great venue for the communication of God's presence or is one place far more likely than the other to lead you into the Holy of Holies? Does preaching connect with, comfort, and challenge your life as a worker, or is there a disconnection between what you hear in church and what you face each day at work?

These are some of the questions addressed in *Grace for the Workplace*. This spiritual gem is theologically grounded and rooted in scripture. It focuses upon the free and undeserved self-communication of God ~ GRACE ~ in our places of work and worship. Pastor Johnson's thought-provoking ideas about the human propensity for law, leadership models, preaching, learning, and the primacy of grace will raise the bar on what you expect from work and from the pulpit. You will be convinced that always and everywhere GRACE IS TRUMP!"

**Keith Perleberg, Roman Catholic Priest
Diocese of Madison, Wisconsin**

ENDNOTES

1 FOR CLERGY AND WORKFORCE

1. Looking up Lectionary on the Internet reveals several different versions but a spot check suggests that they are all basically the same.

2. See Merton P. Strommen, *A Study of Generations* (Minneapolis: Augsburg, 1972) p.369. In the "Salvation by Works" scale, the reference is Item One.

2 TWO FOUNDATIONS

1. John Simmons and William J. Mares, *Working Together* (New York: Knopf, 1983), p. 160.

2. Dietrich Bonhoeffer is perhaps the best known for lifting up this world-centered view of God at work, but he was preceded in this concept by Richard Niebuhr and Walter Rauschenbusch..

3. This study was designed by the author and completed while serving as the Project Manager of Studies for the Parish Services Division of the Lutheran Church in America in 1984. It was reported under the title of "The Sunday/Monday Faith and Work Study."

4. This conference was held in Milwaukee in June 1982. The observation of John Raines appeared in the *Religion and Labor Newsletter* published on that occasion.

5. These words are those of Gustaf Wingren, a theologian from Sweden who wrote them in a forward to the author's book, *Grace: God's Work Ethic*, published by Judson Press in 1985.

6. See Max Weber, *The Protestant Ethic and the Spirit of Capitalism* (New York: Scribner, 1958), p. 80.

3 NEWS FROM THE PEWS

1. Don Chrysostomus Baur, *John Chrysostom And His Times* (Westminster, Maryland: Newman Press, 1959) Vol. I, p. 231.

2. Ibid, Vol. II, p. 86.

3. Ibid., Vol. I, p. 234.

4. D. Martyn Lloyd-Jones, *Preaching and Preachers* (London: Hodder and Stoughton, 1973), p. 52.

5. Dietrich Ritschl, *A Theology of Proclamation* (Richmond: John Knox Press, 1960), p. 129.

6. "How to Teach for Retention," Chart III (Minneapolis: Augustana Board of Parish Education, 1960)

7. Carl H. Weaver, *Listening: Process and Behavior* (Indianapolis: Dobbs-Merrill, 1972) pp. 34-59.

8. See Sidney James French, *Accent on Teaching* (New York: Harper, 1954), Chapter One, "The Thought Process of Students in Discussion" by Benjamin S. Bloom, pp. 22-46.

9. This experiment was conducted to fulfill my requirements for a Doctor of Ministry degree at Andover Newton Theological School in 1976.

10. Aurelius Augustine, *On Christian Doctrine*, Book 4, Chapter 20, Section 39, present in English in *Nicene and Post-Nicene Fathers,* V. II, Philip Schaff, ed., (Buffalo: Christian Literature Co., 1887), p. 588.

4 HOLDING LAY FEET TO THE FIRE

1. Joseph F. Girzone, *Joshua* (New York: Doubleday, 1994) p. 98. This is the first of Girzone's books first published in 1983 by Richelieu Court. This and other books of his can be obtained in local libraries and book stores.

2. Ibid., p. 48.

3. Ibid., p. 292

4. Karen Anderson, *A History of God* (New York: Alfred A. Knopf, 1993), p. 158. This appears in her chapter on Islam but she refers to both male

Muslims and male Christians as "hijacking" their religion.

5. In the tenth chapter of the Book of Acts (verse 34-35) the writer reveals something of Peter's law orientation and theology when he is quoted as follows: "I truly understand that God shows no partiality, but in every nation anyone who fears him and *does what is right* is acceptable to him..."

6. Martin Luther, *A Commentary on St. Paul's Epistle to the Galatians* (Philadelphia: Quaker City Publishing House, 1875), p. 225.

7. This quotation was appended to a question on the work ethic answered by a pastor in the "Sunday/Monday Study" noted in a previous chapter as having involved the writer.

8. David Bleakly, *In Place of Work...The Sufficient Society* (London, SCM Press, 1981), p. 59

5 A MEMO TO THE CEO

1. Dietrich Bonhoeffer, *Ethics* (New York: Macmillan, 1955), pp. 64 and 281.

2. Bonhoeffer, *Letters and Papers from Prison* (New York, Macmillan, 1972), p. 360

6 THE BOSS AND THE FOREMAN

1. This scenario is an adaptation from a Broadway Play in the Sixties. Before passing sentence on a murderer, the judge left his bench, walked to the convicted one and said, "You are free to go." The judge then took the murderer's place, and in the crowd, which had served as the jury, a mixture of applause and catcalls erupted.

7 UNDER NEW MANAGEMENT

1. Jack Miles, *God: A Biography* (New York: Vintage Books, 1996) p. 46.

2. Ibid., p. 291

8 GRACE IN THREE WORK AREAS

1. See Karel von Wolferin, *The Enigma of Japanese Power* (New York: Knopf, 1989), p. 88.

2. John Simmons and William J. Mares, *Working Together* (New York, Alfred Knopf, Inc., 1983) p. 160.

3. Ibid., p. 215.

4. Pehr Gyllenhammar, *People at Work* (Reading, MA: Addison-Wesley, 1977) p. 162.

5. "Steel Jacks Up Its Productivity," *Business Week* (October 12, 1981), p. 86.

6. This first appeared in an article by Jim Fuller, entitled "Workers Gaining Voice in Job Policy," in the Minneapolis *Tribune* (July 8, 1979, p. 1D. However, the writer used it in his book *Grace: God's Work Ethic* (Valley Forge, Judson Press, 1985.

9 GRACE AND CAPITALISM

1. Dietrich Bonhoeffer, *The Cost of Discipleship*, (London, SCM Press, 1939), p. 38.

2. Dietrich Bonhoeffer, *Life Together* (New York: Harper & Brothers, 1954) p. 110.

3. Ibid., p. 39.

4. David E. Roberts, *Existentialism and Religious Belief* (New York: Oxford University Press, 1957), p. 123.

5. See Stephen Laszlo, "Sin in the Holy Church of God," in *Council Speeches of Vatican II* (Glen Rock, N.J.: Paulist Press, 1964), p. 46.

6. Tony Hillerman, *Finding Moon* (New York: HarperCollins, 1995), pp. 76-77. Mr. Hillerman is the author of mystery stories involving the Navajo Indians in the Southwest. His sensitivity to religious beliefs is always a part of his stories.

7. This appeared in a cartoon in *The Boston Globe* in 1966 on the editorial page, under the caption, "How long does it take to earn $8,840," the minimum wage for that year. For the reference to Ken Lewis, see Sasha

Talcott, "Bank of America Chief paid 20m," *The Boston Globe,* April 24, 2004, p. F1.

8. Kenneth D. Campbell, "Malden Mills owner applies religious ethics to business," *Tech Talk*, Cambridge, Ma., MIT News Office, April 16, 1997.

10 WHAT UNCONDITIONL GRACE IMPLIES

1. Copies of these Gospels are found in *The Lost Books of the Bible* (New York: Bell, 1979). The board story is in "Joseph's Bad Carpentry," pp. 53-54.

2. The pedophile issue is something else. Children need to be protected, but putting clergy in prison or paying millions in damages doesn't do that, especially when it is twenty years after the fact. Pedophilia is basically a sickness. It needs to be identified in theological schools, before ordination sanctions it. At that point grace would be operative. Grace hardly enters into it where lawyers and "victims" are using the situation for acquiring material wealth decades later.

3. Wesley Shrader, *Yeshua's Diary* (Valley Forge, Judson Press, 1967) p. 74.

4. Dietrich Bonhoeffer, *Life Together* (New York, Harper, 1954), p. 27.

5. The movie setting is a desolate stretch of Danish coastline, not a Norwegian fjord. The guest's speech is found on page forty in the book written by the well-known author Karen Blixen under the pen name Isak Dinesen . See *Babette's Feast and Other Anecdotes of Destiny* (New York: Vintage Books,1988). It was first published in 1953.

11 THE PULPIT WORKPLACE

1. Ludwig Feuerbach, *The Essence of Christianity* (London: Ludgate Hill, 1881), p. 265. Translated into English by George Elliot (New York: Harper, 1957).

NOTES & IDEAS

executive sessions 59

F

Fafner Bearing Company 112
faith alone 109
fallacies 25
family 58
father 34
fear 13, 16, 40, 45, 58, 72, 73,
   88, 94, 95, 109
Feuerbach, Ludwig 109
Feuerstein, Aaron 86
forgiveness 8, 16, 54, 70, 73, 75,
   76, 79, 80, 83, 87, 88, 89, 92, 93,
   94, 97, 99, 107
free will 20

G

General Motors Corporation 59
Girzone, Joseph 35
Gospel 4, 7, 10, 34, 37, 49, 51,
   91, 93, 94, 97, 113, 114
grace (cheap) 8, 79, 93, 107, 108,
   114
grace (definition) 2
grace (justification by) 37
grace (suspect) 17
grace alone 109, 110, 113, 114
Greenleaf, Robert 44
Gyllenhammar, Peter 72

H

Hamilton Corporation 57, 63
Hayes Associates 40
hierarchy 35, 36, 40, 41, 72, 96
homiletical transubstantiation 25
hypocrisy 81

I

Ignatius of Antioch 36
Indulgence 37
interpretation 65, 106, 109

J

Japan 12, 44, 70, 106
jealous 49, 50
Jennings, Peter 80
Jesus 7, 12, 19, 31, 34, 35, 38,
   40, 42, 44, 72, 78, 80, 84, 91, 93,
   94, 95, 96, 97, 104, 108
Jesus (Foreman) 49
Jesus and Paul (TV show) 80
John the Baptist 97
Jones/Laughlin Steel Corporation 72
Joseph 91
Joshua 35
Judas 94

K

kerygma 94
Kirkegaard, Soren 82
Korah's rebellion 60

L

law 3, 5, 7, 8, 9, 10, 13, 16, 17,
   29, 31, 35, 36, 37, 40, 42, 45, 56,
   70, 72, 88, 94, 97, 99, 100, 103, 108,
   113, 114
law (tyranny) 18
learning 26
lectionary 4, 7, 9, 103, 108
Lectionary, Revised Common 4
Lewis, Ken 86
listening 27, 39, 43
Lloyd-Jones, Martin 25
lording it over 34, 58, 72, 105
Luther (movie) 8
Luther, Martin 4, 6, 8, 19, 37, 38,
   42, 82, 106, 109, 113, 114

M

Malden Textile Mills 86
management (enforcer) 15
McPherson, Rene 11, 13, 73, 98
mercy 57, 61, 62, 64, 73, 97, 104,

trust 49, 51, 56, 58, 59, 63, 95,
  96
twelve 14, 31, 32, 34, 35
tyranny 29, 31, 41

U

Uncle Ed 86
unemployment 41, 59, 85
union protest 60
union steward 52, 88
unmerited grace 2, 3, 8, 13, 24, 36,
  39, 42, 54, 64, 69, 71, 73, 76, 77,
  85, 87, 102, 110

V

Vietnam War 113

W

Weber, Max 19
women (role of) 36
Word 23, 24, 25, 31, 37, 38, 39,
  46, 73, 97
wrath 10, 38, 52, 57, 60, 62, 63,
  64, 67, 94, 97, 104, 105

Jesus, King of Israel
Samaritan Blood and the Kingdom at Shiloh

by J. S. Tyson
Fellow of the University of British Columbia

Publication Date: April 25, 2005

A refreshingly unique insight into the Gospel of John,
offering a paradigm shift in the quest for the historical Jesus.

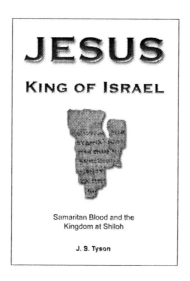

ISBN 0-9735341-5-X
6x9 Paperback 336pp (289pp + Appendix, Bibliography & Index)
4 maps, various diagrams/tables
US$22.95

www.eccenova.com

Printed in the United States
27527LVS00001B/301